I0820204

A KID'S GUIDE to the WORLD through FACTS and FIGURES

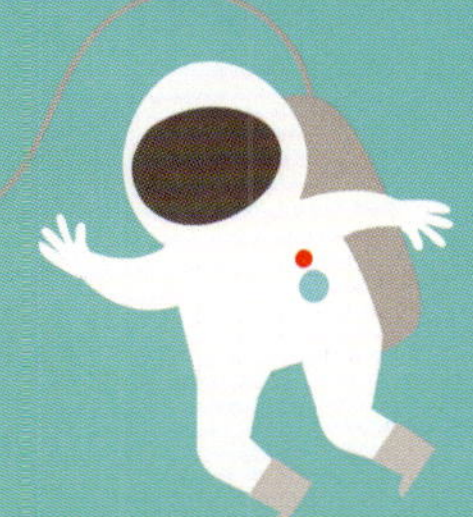

Researched and written by
Susan Martineau

Designed and illustrated by
Vicky Barker

Sky Pony Press
New York, NY

 • 10 9 8 7 6 5 4 3 2 1 • Production by Madeleine Ehm • ISBN: 978-1-5107-8143-6
Ebook: 978-1-5107-8367-6 • Manufactured in China, November 2024
This product conforms to CPSIA 2008

CONTENTS

6-50 THE WORLD IN FACTS

51-96 THE WORLD IN FIGURES

GREEN THINGS IN THE RAINFOREST

TROPICAL RAINFOREST

This grows around the central part of the Earth. It is always hot and humid and contains an amazing variety of plants and animals.

EMERALD TREE BOA

When this snake is young it is not green but reddish-orange. It stays up in the trees where it feeds on rats, lizards and monkeys.

GREAT GREEN MACAW

Macaws are the biggest of the world's parrots. They use their strong, hooked beaks to crack nuts and seeds.

WHITE-LIPPED TREE FROG

This frog can be bright green or brownish green, but it always has a white bottom lip. It has big feet with large webbed toes and is a fantastic tree-climber. Male frogs can also bark like a dog!

PRAYING MANTIS

This bug looks like an alien with its triangular head and massive eyes. Its spiky front legs are folded so that it looks as if it is praying.

TUCUNARE FISH

This fierce fish is a really determined hunter. It does not give up, even if it misses its prey the first time around. Then it usually swallows it whole.

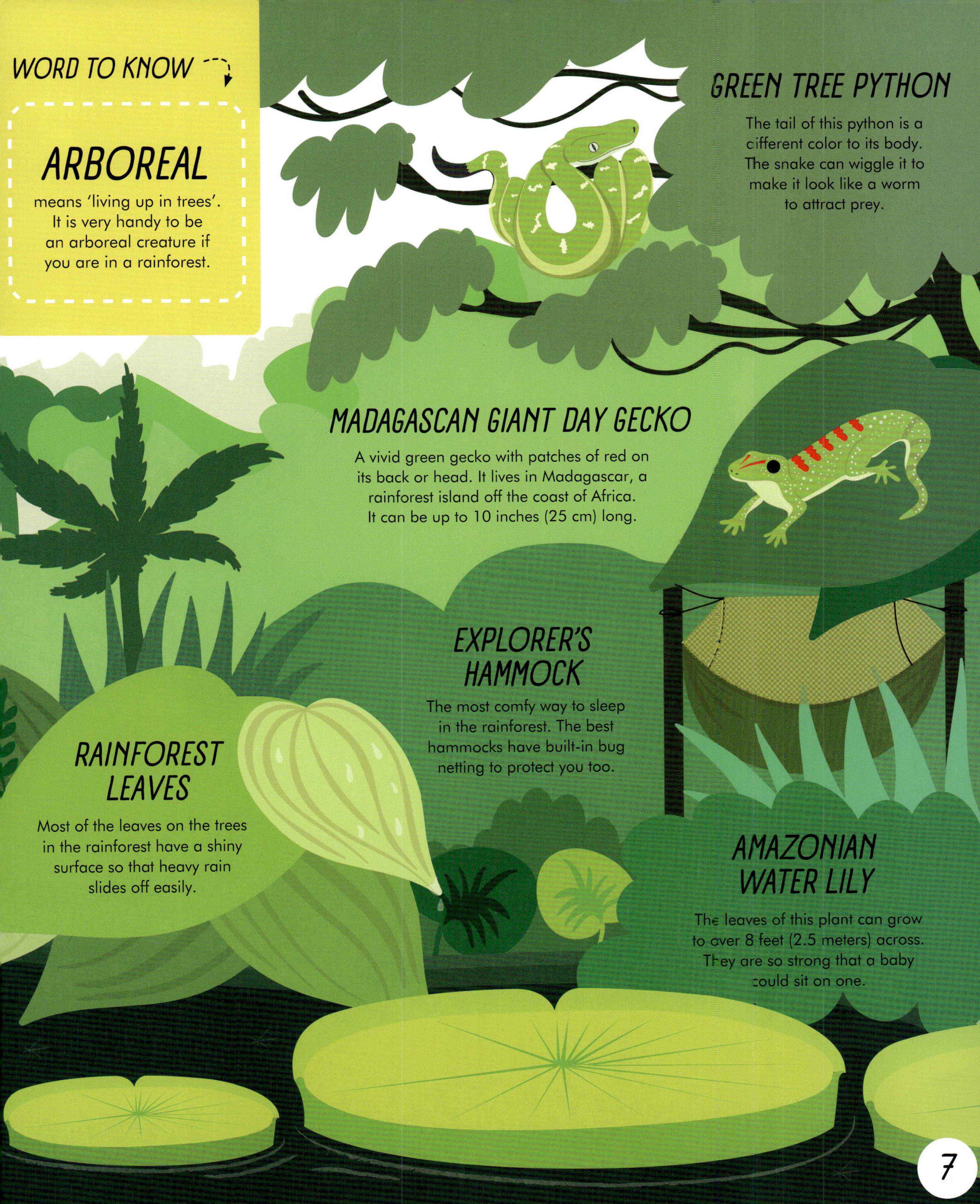
WORD TO KNOW
ARBOREAL
means 'living up in trees'. It is very handy to be an arboreal creature if you are in a rainforest.
GREEN TREE PYTHON
The tail of this python is a different color to its body. The snake can wiggle it to make it look like a worm to attract prey.
MADAGASCAN GIANT DAY GECKO
A vivid green gecko with patches of red on its back or head. It lives in Madagascar, a rainforest island off the coast of Africa. It can be up to 10 inches (25 cm) long.
EXPLORER'S HAMMOCK
The most comfy way to sleep in the rainforest. The best hammocks have built-in bug netting to protect you too.
RAINFOREST LEAVES
Most of the leaves on the trees in the rainforest have a shiny surface so that heavy rain slides off easily.
AMAZONIAN WATER LILY
The leaves of this plant can grow to over 8 feet (2.5 meters) across. They are so strong that a baby could sit on one.

AT HOME IN SPACE

INTERNATIONAL SPACE STATION

A working laboratory that is home to astronauts from many different countries. It is bigger than a six-bedroomed house and orbits about 250 miles (402 km) above Earth.

VIEW FROM SPACE

The crew can see the sun setting and rising 16 times a day as the space station orbits the Earth once every 90 minutes. The views are spectacular.

STRAPS AND FASTENINGS

Everything, even really heavy objects, floats in the space station because the force of gravity that normally pulls things down to Earth is not very strong in space. Straps, fastenings and Velcro are essential to keep things where you can find them.

SPACEWALK

This is when an astronaut goes outside the space station to repair something or to carry out an experiment. A space walk usually lasts between five to eight hours depending on the job that needs doing.

SPACE MEALS

Food is ready to eat from specially prepared packages. No plates are needed. Sometimes a cargo vehicle brings in fresh fruit, but there's no pizza delivery in space!

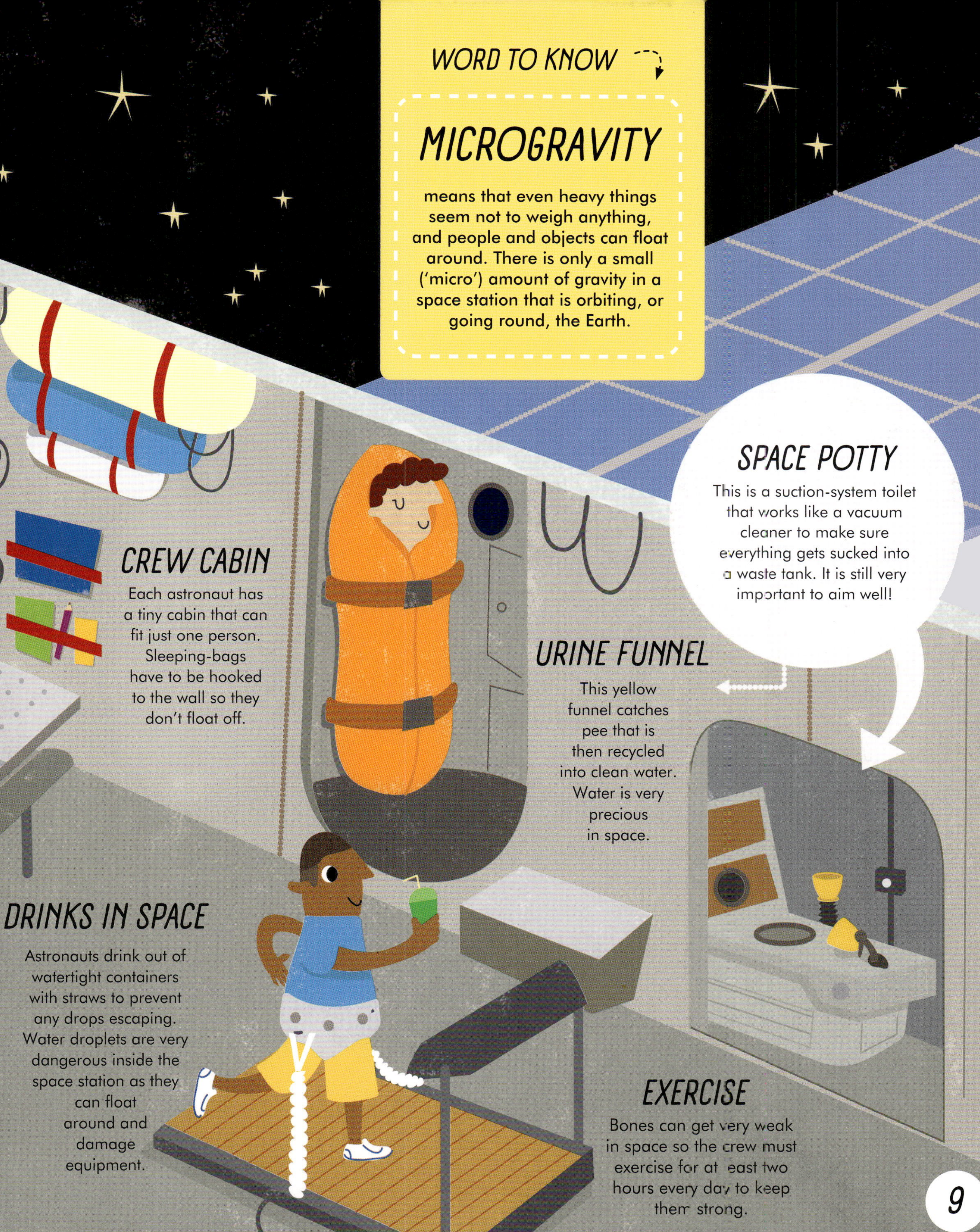
WORD TO KNOW
MICROGRAVITY
means that even heavy things seem not to weigh anything, and people and objects can float around. There is only a small ('micro') amount of gravity in a space station that is orbiting, or going round, the Earth.
SPACE POTTY
This is a suction-system toilet that works like a vacuum cleaner to make sure everything gets sucked into a waste tank. It is still very important to aim well!
CREW CABIN
Each astronaut has a tiny cabin that can fit just one person. Sleeping-bags have to be hooked to the wall so they don't float off.
URINE FUNNEL
This yellow funnel catches pee that is then recycled into clean water. Water is very precious in space.
DRINKS IN SPACE
Astronauts drink out of watertight containers with straws to prevent any drops escaping. Water droplets are very dangerous inside the space station as they can float around and damage equipment.
EXERCISE
Bones can get very weak in space so the crew must exercise for at least two hours every day to keep them strong.

BRAVE EXPLORERS OF THE WORLD

AMELIA EARHART

She was known as the 'Winged Legend'. In 1932 she became the first woman to fly across the Atlantic on her own. But in 1937 she disappeared while making an attempt to fly round the world.

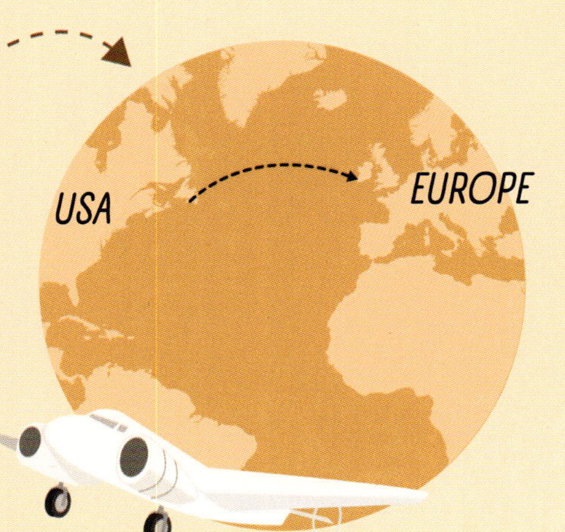

JOHN CABOT

In 1497 Cabot and his sons set off in a tiny ship called the *Matthew* with just 18 men. They sailed from Bristol, England to the American coast, probably landing at Cape Breton in Nova Scotia. At first Cabot thought it was China!

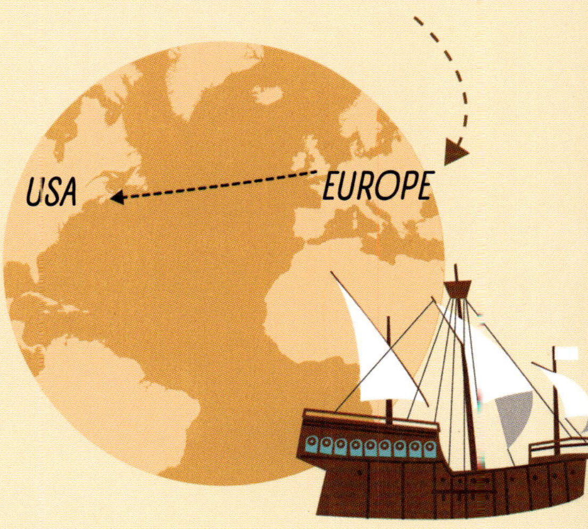

PERU

POLYNESIA

THOR HEYERDAHL

He wanted to prove that people in ancient times could have sailed from South America to the Polynesian islands in the Pacific Ocean. In 1947 he set off in a simple wooden raft called the *Kon-Tiki*. He made it despite shark attacks and fresh water running out.

ROALD AMUNDSEN

The Norwegian polar explorer was not only the first person to reach the South Pole in 1911, but he also found a route from the Arctic Ocean to the Pacific Ocean called the Northwest Passage.

JACQUES PICCARD AND DON WALSH

They became the first people to reach the deepest-known part of the ocean in their special submarine called a bathyscaphe. In 1960 they went 7 miles down (10,915 meters) to Challenger Deep in the Mariana Trench of the Pacific Ocean.

FERDINAND MAGELLAN

The Portuguese explorer set out in 1519 with five ships and about 260 men. Only one ship and 18 men made it all the way round the world, arriving home three years later in 1522. Sadly, Magellan himself did not survive the trip.

MARY KINGSLEY

During 1893 and 1894 this intrepid woman roamed the forests of the Congo in West Africa on foot and paddled up the river in a dug-out canoe. She collected specimens for the Natural History Museum in London.

NIGERIA

GERMAN CAMEROON

Route on foot

Route by canoe

FRENCH CONGO

YURI GAGARIN

He was the first human to journey into space. On 12 April 1961 his spaceship *Vostok* was launched from Russia. It took Gagarin one hour and 48 minutes to fly right round the Earth.

BURKE AND WILLS

In 1860 Robert Burke and William Wills set out to cross Australia from south to north. They reached the swamps of the north coast, but had to turn round as their supplies were running out. Sadly they both died on the journey back.

WORD TO KNOW

CIRCUMNAVIGATE

means to travel all the way round something, in this case the world.

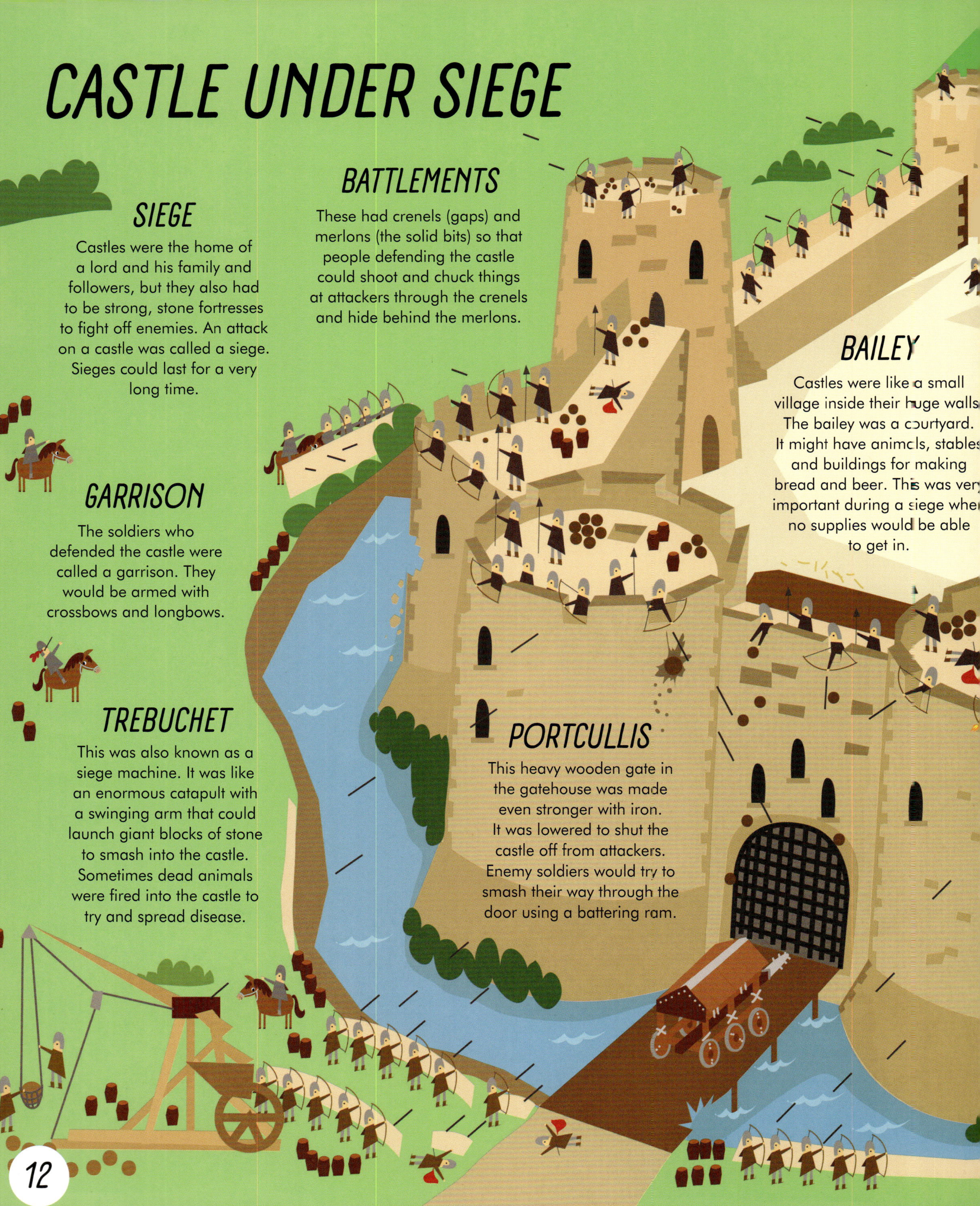

CASTLE UNDER SIEGE

SIEGE

Castles were the home of a lord and his family and followers, but they also had to be strong, stone fortresses to fight off enemies. An attack on a castle was called a siege. Sieges could last for a very long time.

BATTLEMENTS

These had crenels (gaps) and merlons (the solid bits) so that people defending the castle could shoot and chuck things at attackers through the crenels and hide behind the merlons.

BAILEY

Castles were like a small village inside their huge walls. The bailey was a courtyard. It might have animals, stables and buildings for making bread and beer. This was very important during a siege when no supplies would be able to get in.

GARRISON

The soldiers who defended the castle were called a garrison. They would be armed with crossbows and longbows.

TREBUCHET

This was also known as a siege machine. It was like an enormous catapult with a swinging arm that could launch giant blocks of stone to smash into the castle. Sometimes dead animals were fired into the castle to try and spread disease.

PORTCULLIS

This heavy wooden gate in the gatehouse was made even stronger with iron. It was lowered to shut the castle off from attackers. Enemy soldiers would try to smash their way through the door using a battering ram.

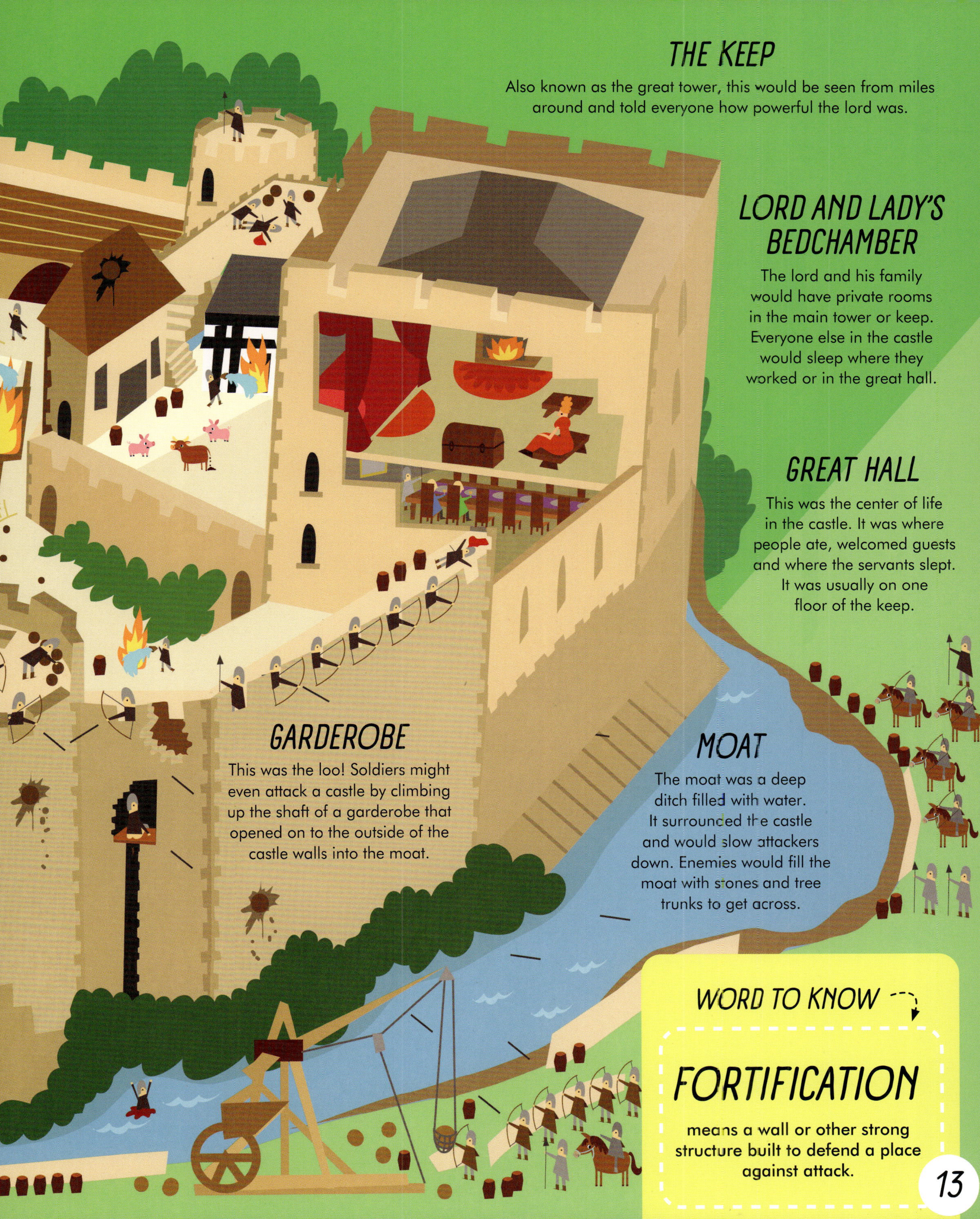

THE KEEP

Also known as the great tower, this would be seen from miles around and told everyone how powerful the lord was.

LORD AND LADY'S BEDCHAMBER

The lord and his family would have private rooms in the main tower or keep. Everyone else in the castle would sleep where they worked or in the great hall.

GREAT HALL

This was the center of life in the castle. It was where people ate, welcomed guests and where the servants slept. It was usually on one floor of the keep.

GARDEROBE

This was the loo! Soldiers might even attack a castle by climbing up the shaft of a garderobe that opened on to the outside of the castle walls into the moat.

MOAT

The moat was a deep ditch filled with water. It surrounded the castle and would slow attackers down. Enemies would fill the moat with stones and tree trunks to get across.

WORD TO KNOW

FORTIFICATION

means a wall or other strong structure built to defend a place against attack.

CLEVER CAMOUFLAGE

CAMOUFLAGE

Most wild creatures are difficult to see because their shape or color helps them blend into where they live. Camouflage can help animals to hide from predators or to hunt for prey.

PRETEND TO BE DEAD

The oakleaf butterfly looks just like a dead leaf when it folds its wings. Even the veins underneath look like those on a leaf. No wonder its other name is dead-leaf butterfly!

FAKE WASP

The wasp beetle pretends to be a wasp with its black and yellow warning stripes. It is handy for protection to look fiercer than you are.

INVISIBLE TOAD

Frogs and toads in the rainforest have to be able to hide from hungry predators. The Asian horned toad can blend in with its surroundings on a bed of rotting leaves.

HIDDEN FAWN

Newborn baby deer have markings on their coats to look like sunlight coming through the leaves in a forest. They keep very still so predators cannot see them.

SPOTTY SHARK

The spotted wobbegong is a type of carpet shark that is flat and patterned pale yellow or greenish brown with spots. This is superb camouflage for lurking on all types of seabed. It will give you a nasty bite if you step on it!

WORD TO KNOW

MIMICRY

is when a creature pretends to be something else to protect itself or to find prey.

ARCTIC FUR

The beautiful arctic fox is dark in the summer and white in the winter snows. Its thick fur even covers the soles of its feet.

SHIMMERING STRIPES

When zebras stand together they are a confusing mass of black and white patterns that make it difficult for a lion to nab one! In the shimmering heat haze of Africa the zebra's stripes blur.

Tiger

INVISIBLE CATS

Tigers, jaguars, ocelots and leopards are all members of the cat family with beautiful camouflage markings. They can blend in with their surroundings to hunt their prey.

OCELOT

COLOR-CHANGE CUTTLEFISH

These are masters of disguise and can change their color and even the texture of their skin to match different types of seabed. They can even disguise themselves as clumps of floating seaweed!

DIGGING INTO ANCIENT TIMES

MIGHTY MESOPOTAMIA

Mesopotamia, or the 'cradle of civilization', was where Iraq is now. Over 5,000 years ago this is where people first started building towns, making laws and using inventions like the wheel and writing.

SUMERIAN MASTER BUILDERS

The Sumerians were the first people to settle in Mesopotamia. They became rich from farming and built huge temples called ziggurats where they would worship their gods.

ANCIENT EGYPTIAN GAME

The Ancient Egyptians enjoyed board games. The most popular one was a bit like chess and called senet. The winner was believed to be protected by the gods. Senet sets have been found in the tombs of pharaohs.

PHOENICIAN TRADERS

The Phoenicians were expert sailors who lived around the shores of the Mediterranean Sea. They travelled around trading gold, jewels, wine, spices and glass in their large ships.

GREEK SCHOOLS

In Ancient Greece only boys went to school. From scenes painted on pottery we can see that they would use a pointed stick, called a stylus, to scratch their lessons on a wax tablet.

ANCIENT CHINESE EMPEROR

The first emperor of China, Qin Shi Huang, brought in standard versions of coins, writing and laws across the land. He also left behind an amazing tomb containing thousands of clay soldiers.

ROMAN ARMY TRICKS

The Romans had the best army in the world. Writings from the time describe one of their battle techniques called the testudo (Latin for 'tortoise'). The soldiers locked their shields together to protect themselves.

ARCHAEOLOGIST

is someone who looks at ancient objects and buildings to find out how people lived in the past. They are like history detectives looking for clues.

MINOAN CRAFTSMEN

The Minoans lived on the Mediterranean island of Crete. You can still visit the remains of one of their palaces called Knossos. Minoans made beautiful wall paintings, pottery and gold jewellery.

VIKING EXPLORATION

Archaeologists can see from the remains of their boats that Viking ships were light and could travel quickly. Vikings were the first people from Europe to sail across the Atlantic Ocean to North America, reaching Canada over a thousand years ago.

MYSTERIOUS OLMECS OF MEXICO

The Olmecs are probably one of the earliest civilizations of Central America. They came before the Mayans and Aztecs. They carved huge stone heads and strange sculptures combining jaguars with human babies.

FANTASTIC FLYING MACHINES

INFLATABLE AIRSHI

An American inventor called Charles Ritchel made the first inflatable airship or dirigible. The pilot sat under a huge bag of gas, turned a hand-crank to make the propeller work and steered using pedals.

MONSTER BALLOON

In 1783, in front of the King of France, the Montgolfier brothers launched a hot-air balloon carrying the first living beings. A duck, a sheep and a rooster flew in a small basket under the balloon.

OTTO'S GLIDER

Otto Lilienthal was a German engineer who invented a wing-flapping glider. He made several successful flights between 1891 and 1896, but sadly died after crashing in 1896.

THE FLYING MONK

In 1010 a monk called Eilmer of Malmesbury made a pair of wings. He attached them to his hands and feet and tried to fly by jumping from a high tower. He managed to go about 650 feet (200 meters) before falling down and breaking both his legs. Ow!

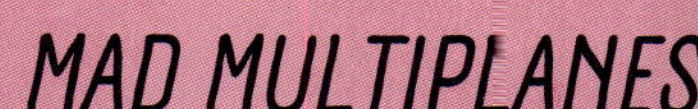

MAD MULTIPLANES

In the early 1900s many inventors came up with the idea of multi-winged airplanes, but most of them would barely leave the ground.

FLYING SAUCER

NASA developed a saucer-shaped, rocket-powered space vehicle that could help in future missions to Mars. Its proper name is a Low-Density Supersonic Decelerator!

WORD TO KNOW

AERONAUTICS

is the science of designing and building aircraft.

MOTORBIKES IN THE SKY

Gyrocopters look like a cross between a motorbike and a helicopter. They can fly lower than most other flying machines and land in very small spaces.

HOT-AIR HISTORY

In 1999 Bertrand Piccard and Brian Jones became the first men to fly around the world in a hot-air balloon. It took them just under 20 days in their amazing high-altitude Breitling Orbiter 3.

WINGSUITS

Modern wingsuits were first invented in the 1990s. They are also called squirrel or birdmen suits. They are very difficult to control and fliers must use a parachute to land safely.

FLYING CAR

The Hall Flying Automobile or Convair 118 was a family car with a plane on top! It did take to the air in 1947, but was wrecked on its third flight.

FORCES IN ACTION

FORCE

A force is a push or a pull. Every day we use force in many different ways. When you push or pull open a door you are applying a force. We use force when we are lifting, bending, stretching or squeezing things.

FORCES IN BALANCE

Forces come in pairs. When a force pushes on something, another one pushes back. The second force is the same strength as the first one. When you lean on a wall your weight pushes on the wall. At the same time the wall is pushing back. Otherwise you would fall through the wall!

FORCE AND MOVEMENT

Force makes things move. It will make things move faster, more slowly, or change direction. When you kick a ball or hit it with a bat you are applying a force.

GRAVITY AND WEIGHT

Gravity is a force that pulls things towards the ground. Gravity pulling us down gives us, and everything around us, weight. When we drop something it is gravity that makes it fall to the ground. When rockets blast off into space they have to go at incredible speeds to break free of the Earth's gravity.

WORD TO KNOW

CENTRIPETAL

is the name given to the force that stops you falling out of your seat when you are on a roller coaster looping the loop. Centripetal force keeps you pressed into your chair.

GRIPPING FORCE

The force produced when two things rub together is called friction. It is a gripping force that is often helpful. Without friction our feet would slip all over the floor and we would fall over. Too much friction can stop machines from working. Oil is added to parts of machines to make less friction between the parts that need to work smoothly together.

AIR FRICTION

If you throw a ball up into the air it has to slide through the air. This causes friction too. This kind of friction is called air resistance. Air resistance can be useful if you are falling to Earth with a parachute, as it will slow you down!

FRICTION AND BIKES!

You need force to make your bike work. Friction helps you and also slows you down.

Friction between the bike and the air slows you down, especially on a windy day!

Friction between brakes and wheels makes the brakes work.

Friction helps your feet grip the pedals.

Friction between the tires and the road helps the wheels to grip, but friction also slows the wheels down.

FRIENDLY DINOSAURS

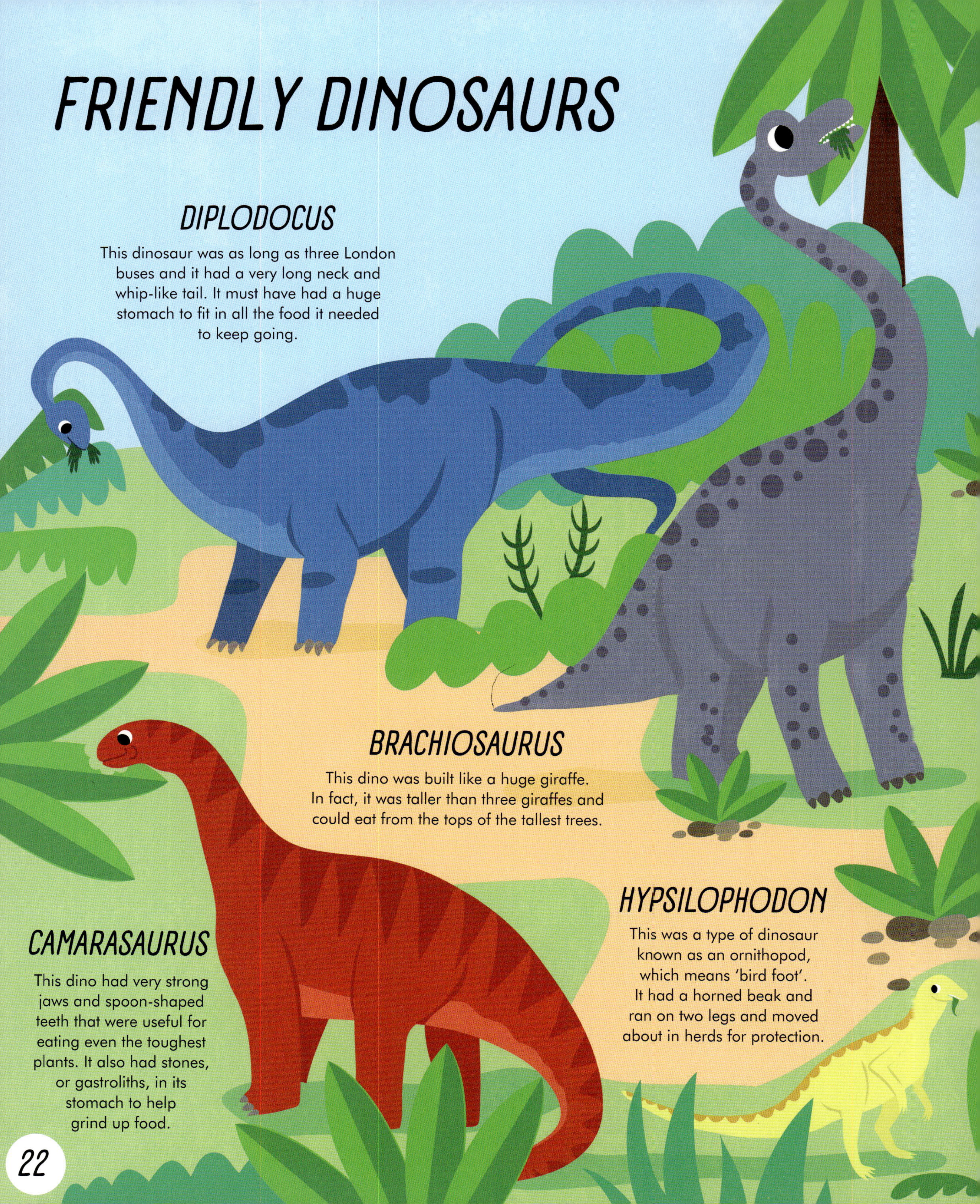

DIPLODOCUS

This dinosaur was as long as three London buses and it had a very long neck and whip-like tail. It must have had a huge stomach to fit in all the food it needed to keep going.

BRACHIOSAURUS

This dino was built like a huge giraffe. In fact, it was taller than three giraffes and could eat from the tops of the tallest trees.

HYPSILOPHODON

This was a type of dinosaur known as an ornithopod, which means 'bird foot'. It had a horned beak and ran on two legs and moved about in herds for protection.

CAMARASAURUS

This dino had very strong jaws and spoon-shaped teeth that were useful for eating even the toughest plants. It also had stones, or gastroliths, in its stomach to help grind up food.

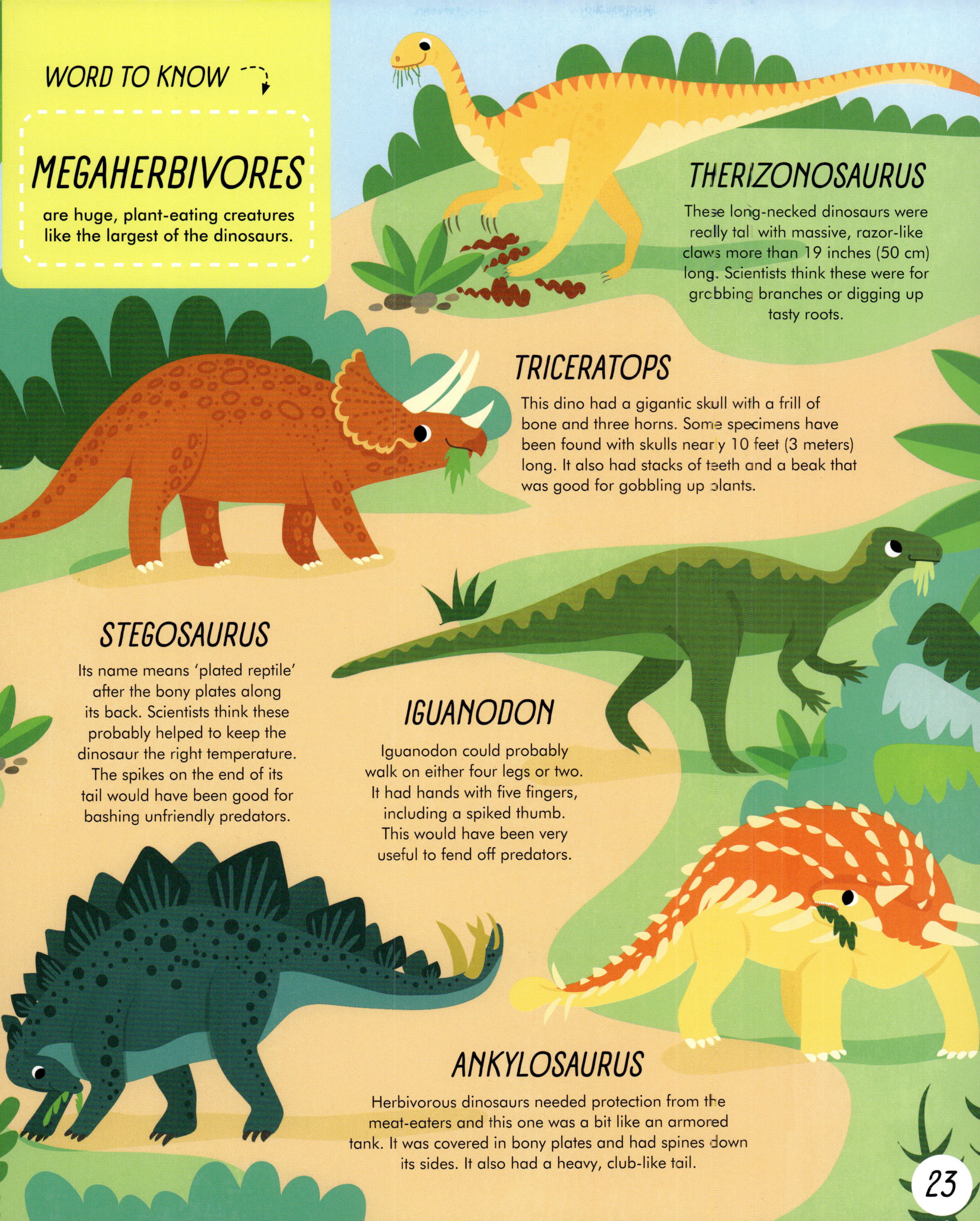

WORD TO KNOW

MEGAHERBIVORES

are huge, plant-eating creatures like the largest of the dinosaurs.

THERIZONOSAURUS

These long-necked dinosaurs were really tall with massive, razor-like claws more than 19 inches (50 cm) long. Scientists think these were for grabbing branches or digging up tasty roots.

TRICERATOPS

This dino had a gigantic skull with a frill of bone and three horns. Some specimens have been found with skulls nearly 10 feet (3 meters) long. It also had stacks of teeth and a beak that was good for gobbling up plants.

STEGOSAURUS

Its name means 'plated reptile' after the bony plates along its back. Scientists think these probably helped to keep the dinosaur the right temperature. The spikes on the end of its tail would have been good for bashing unfriendly predators.

IGUANODON

Iguanodon could probably walk on either four legs or two. It had hands with five fingers, including a spiked thumb. This would have been very useful to fend off predators.

ANKYLOSAURUS

Herbivorous dinosaurs needed protection from the meat-eaters and this one was a bit like an armored tank. It was covered in bony plates and had spines down its sides. It also had a heavy, club-like tail.

GENTLE GIANTS UNDER THE SEA

BLUE WHALE

The blue whale can grow as long as a basketball court and is the largest animal ever to have lived on Earth. It weighs as much as 33 elephants and its blood vessels are so wide that a human could swim through them.

WHALE SHARK

Luckily for divers this biggest fish in the world only eats plankton and small fish. The largest one reported so far was 61 feet (18.8 meters) long. Each one has a different pattern of yellow spots that helps researchers keep track of them.

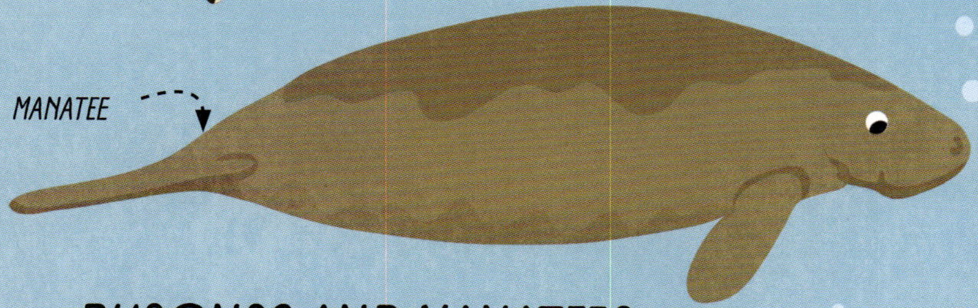

MANATEE

DUGONG

DUGONGS AND MANATEES

Long-ago stories about mermaids may be based on sailors seeing these shy and gentle creatures. They are also sometimes called 'sea-cows' because they graze on underwater grasses.

WORD TO KNOW
CETACEAN
is the word for a sea mammal that has to come up to the surface to breathe. Cetology is the study of whales, dolphins and porpoises.
NARWHAL
This amazing creature looks like a cross between a unicorn and a whale. The males have a huge tusk that is actually a very overgrown tooth. Some narwhals even have two of them.
BASKING SHARK
This mysterious but gentle creature feeds on plankton with its huge mouth. It can filter an Olympic swimming-pool's worth of water in two hours and can grow as long as a double-decker bus.
GIANT CLAM
These multi-colored clams are the largest molluscs on Earth and can grow up to 4 feet (1.2 meters) across. No two clams are the same color and they can live for up to 100 years. They open and close far too slowly to trap any divers!
HUMPHEAD WRASSE
An enormous coral reef fish that has a weird bump on its forehead. It can live for up to 30 years and change from being female to male and back again. It is really friendly to divers and will come up to be patted just like a dog.
LEATHERBACK TURTLE
This is the largest of the sea turtles and it has a leathery, rather than hard, shell. It eats a huge amount of jellyfish and sometimes mistakes discarded plastic bags for a tasty meal. This can be deadly for these endangered giants of the sea.

GLOW-IN-THE-DARK CREATURES

HEADLAMP BEETLE

A fantastic beetle with two glowing green lights on its back and an orange one that 'switches' on underneath the creature when it is about to take off.

FIREFLIES

These are not flies but beetles from the same family as glow-worms. They can fly and look like lots of fairy lights twinkling in the trees. Males flash at night and, if a female is impressed, she will flash back.

GLOW-WORMS

These are not really worms at all, but bioluminescent beetles with glowing tummies. The females glow to attract a mate and also to tell predators that glow-worms taste revolting.

CHIMPANZEE FIRE

Many kinds of fungi or mushrooms glow in the dark and this one is found in the forests of West and Central Africa. The fungi glow as they clean up the forest floor by eating dead leaves and vegetation.

TOXIC MILLIPEDES

In the mountains of California you can see greenish-blue millipedes glowing at night. Scientists think they do this as a warning to predators that they are not good to eat. They are very poisonous.

WORD TO KNOW

BIOLUMINESCENCE

is light made by living organisms to attract attention, frighten enemies, use as a disguise, or to find prey in the dark.

VAMPIRE SQUID

This scary-sounding creature can make a light show of flashing lights to scare off predators or attract prey. It lives really deep down in the ocean and has big, bright eyes too.

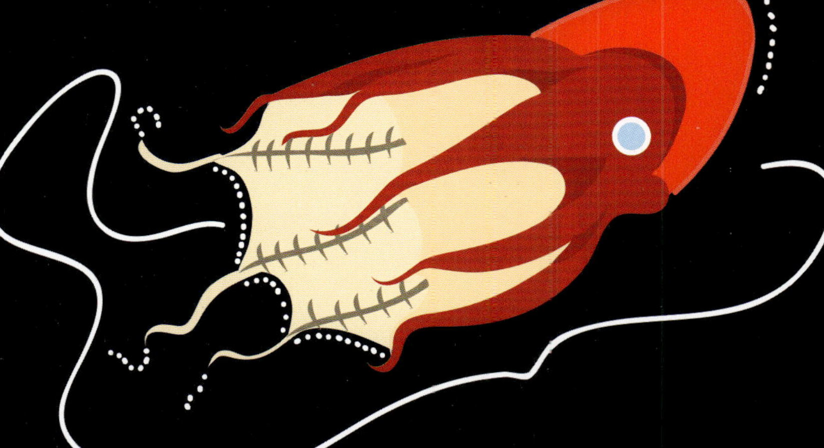

DEEP-SEA SHARKS

These sharks not only glow in the dark, but also have eyes that are adapted to take in as much light as possible down in the depths of the ocean. It means being able to spot each other, catch food and avoid predators.

WAVES OF LIGHT

Tiny, microscopic plants and animals in the sea, called plankton, can make the surface of the ocean glow and glint like a magical sea of light.

CRYSTAL JELLYFISH

Many jellyfish glow in the dark. When crystal jellyfish are disturbed they light up with a green glow around the rim of their bell shapes.

ANGLERFISH

A deep-sea fish that goes fishing with a glowing 'fishing rod' It has a spine sticking up from the middle of its head that it can wriggle to look like bait. Then it grabs its prey with its huge mouth and long, pointed teeth.

HIGH-SPEED ANIMALS

RACEHORSE OF THE BUG WORLD

The lady bug is a very speedy bug. Scientists have found that ladybirds can travel at 37 mph (60 kph). That is as fast as a racehorse.

SUPER SWIFTS

Swifts are very well named, as they are superfast insect-eaters. Their wings are long and curved and the birds spend most of their time in the air. In fact they can even sleep on the wing.

CHARGING RHINO!

Black rhinos are huge creatures, but they are surprisingly fast on their feet. They can turn really quickly and reach speeds of 34 mph (55 kph)

SPEED ON SIX LEGS

Tiger beetles are really fierce hunters with long legs. Compared to their body size, it is like a human running at 480 mph (770 kph).

KILLER KICKERS

Ostriches are the world's largest bird. They cannot fly but can sprint at 45 mph (70 kph) and keep going at this speed for 30 minutes. Their legs are so strong that one kick can kill a human.

SPEEDY SWIMMER

The gentoo penguin cannot fly but it is probably the fastest swimming bird in the world. It can reach speeds of up to 22 mph (36 kph) and is better than other penguins at diving too.

KANGAROO STAMINA

Kangaroos are the only large animals that get about by hopping, but it does not stop them covering a lot of ground. Red kangaroos can keep going at 25 mph (40 kph) for about 1.2 miles (2 km).

WORD TO KNOW

VELOCITY

means the speed and direction of an object or living creature.

HIGH-SPEED HUNTER

The peregrine falcon can dive at lightning speed to pounce on prey. When it dives or 'stoops' like this it can reach the incredible speed of 200 mph (320 kph)

LARGE BUT FAST

Wildebeests are part of the antelope family. They need to be able to move fast to escape from predators like lions and wild dogs. Calves can walk within minutes of birth and adults can reach speeds of 50 mph (80 kph) in an emergency.

TOP SPRINTER

The cheetah is the fastest animal on land. In 2012 a cheetah called Sarah was timed at Cincinnati Zoo running 100 meters in 5.95 seconds. Usain Bolt's record for the same distance is 9.58 seconds!

FAST FISH

It is hard to measure the speed of fish, but the sailfish has been estimated to jet through the water at nearly the same speed as a cheetah on land. It can flatten the huge fin on its back to be as streamlined as possible.

INGENIOUS HOMES FOR HUMANS

PALACE IN THE SKY

The stunning Summer Palace at Wadi Dhahr in Yemen was built on top of a huge rock in the 1920s. The owner could look down on everyone else!

TREEHOUSE PEOPLE

The Koroway tribe in Papua, Indonesia build treehouses up to 98 feet (30 meters) up in the jungle. Climbing the stairs means using a notched tree-trunk.

HOUSES ON A LAKE

Houses on Lake Inle in Myanmar are made of bamboo and stand like islands on wooden stilts in the water. They have floating gardens and fields. Children here learnto swim before they can walk.

PORTABLE HOUSES

The nomads of Mongolia have lived in yurts for thousands of years. These are made from a lattice made of willow or birch wood covered with thick felt. They can be taken down and put up really quickly.

LIVING ON THE SEABED

Deep-sea homes for humans are still really a dream of the future. Most of the people who have spent any time living deep down on the seabed are scientists in special units for research and exploration.

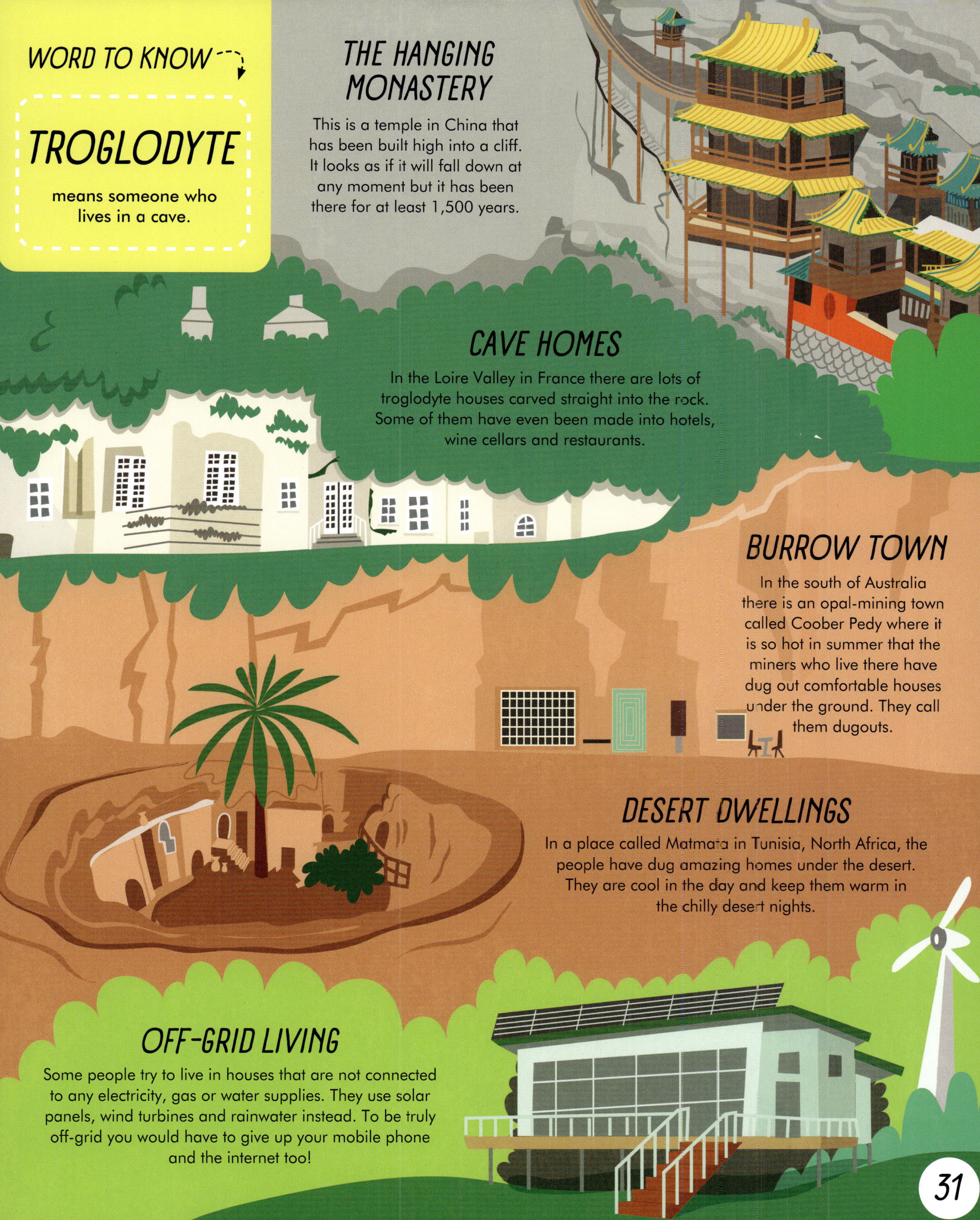

WORD TO KNOW

TROGLODYTE

means someone who lives in a cave.

THE HANGING MONASTERY

This is a temple in China that has been built high into a cliff. It looks as if it will fall down at any moment but it has been there for at least 1,500 years.

CAVE HOMES

In the Loire Valley in France there are lots of troglodyte houses carved straight into the rock. Some of them have even been made into hotels, wine cellars and restaurants.

BURROW TOWN

In the south of Australia there is an opal-mining town called Coober Pedy where it is so hot in summer that the miners who live there have dug out comfortable houses under the ground. They call them dugouts.

DESERT DWELLINGS

In a place called Matmata in Tunisia, North Africa, the people have dug amazing homes under the desert. They are cool in the day and keep them warm in the chilly desert nights.

OFF-GRID LIVING

Some people try to live in houses that are not connected to any electricity, gas or water supplies. They use solar panels, wind turbines and rainwater instead. To be truly off-grid you would have to give up your mobile phone and the internet too!

POWERING THE PLANET

ENERGY FROM THE SUN

Heat and light from the Sun take just over 8 minutes to reach the Earth. Plants and trees use the energy in sunlight to make their own food.

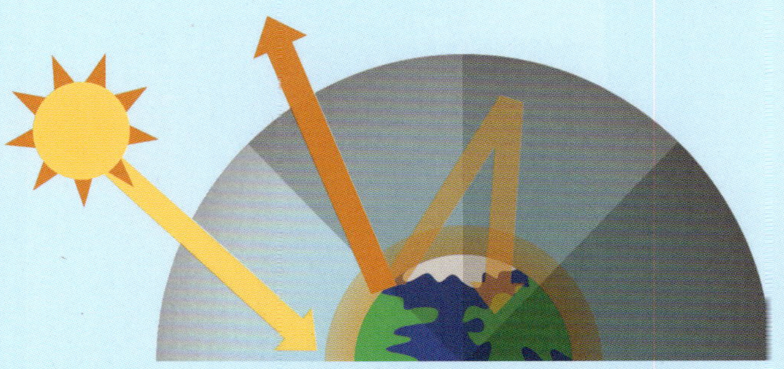

GREENHOUSE GAS

Oil, coal and gas will not last for ever. Burning them makes a gas called carbon dioxide that traps the Sun's heat near Earth, creating what is called the Greenhouse Effect. Our climate is changing because of this and we must find ways of slowing it down.

TIDAL ENERGY

The tide changes twice a day and the movement of the water can be used to turn generators that create electricity without producing harmful gases.

WATER POWER

Hydro-electricity is made by building a dam across a river or lake and then forcing the water down tunnels to turn turbines to make electricity. No harmful gases are created, but building a dam totally changes the environment nearby.

FOSSIL FUELS

Fossil fuels like oil, coal and gas were formed millions of years ago from the remains of dead plants and animals. Using them to make electricity and as fuel for cars causes pollution and the Greenhouse Effect.

WIND POWER

A wind turbine has propellers that turn in the wind to drive a machine called a generator that can make electricity. They do not make greenhouse gases, but need lots of wind and some people really do not like the look of them near their houses.

WORDS TO KNOW

RENEWABLE

energy comes from things that do not run out, like the Sun or the sea.

NON-RENEWABLE

energy comes from sources that will run out. We cannot make any more of them.

NUCLEAR POWER

Uranium ore is made into a metal that can make a huge amount of electricity. The disadvantage is that it produces very dangerous radioactive waste that has to be stored very carefully.

FRACKING

Water, sand and chemicals are injected into shale rock to 'fracture' it and release the gas and oil inside it. There is a worry that the chemicals may be harmful, the process uses loads of water and it may cause small earthquakes.

SOLAR POWER

Solar panels, or photovoltaic cells, make electricity from the power of the Sun. The Sun will not run out soon, and solar panels can even produce power when it is cloudy.

BIOMASS ENERGY

Electricity can be made from burning wood, plants and our old rubbish. It is a good way of using up waste, but burning it creates greenhouse gases. Growing trees to burn also takes up room where crops might be planted to feed people.

SPECIAL EFFECTS IN THE SKY

SPIDER LIGHTNING

This kind of lightning appears to crawl out of a cloud during a thunderstorm. It spreads across the sky like the branches of a tree. It is also called an 'anvil crawler'. Anvil clouds are thunderclouds.

SOLAR ECLIPSE

Sometimes the Moon blocks out the light from the Sun. A total eclipse means that all of the light is blocked and the sky goes dark. All you can see of the Sun is glowing white gases like a halo around the black circle of the Moon. (You must never look at the Sun without eye protection.)

FOG BOWS

These look like the ghosts of rainbows. They are almost white and not colored like rainbows because the water droplets in the mist and fog are too small to turn the light into separate colors.

CONTRAILS

These are man-made clouds of ice crystals that form when water droplets in the air condense and freeze on particles in plane exhaust. Some of them last longer than others.

WORDS TO KNOW

CREPUSCULE

means the time of day just after sunset. Other words for it are dusk or twilight.

THE MILKY WAY

The Milky Way is our home galaxy. There are billions of galaxies in the Universe with gigantic numbers of stars in each one. On dark, clear nights it is possible to see the Milky Way looking like a wide band of white dust stretching across the sky.

AURORA BOREALIS

This is a wonderful show of colored lights in the night sky also known as the Northern Lights as they are most common in Arctic regions. They are caused by tiny pieces from the Sun crashing into the Earth's atmosphere high above the North Pole.

MOON HALO

Ice crystals in clouds high up above the rth can make the Moon look as if it has a lo around it. A Moon halo can often be a sign of stormy weather to come.

LUNAR ECLIPSE

This is when the Earth comes between the Sun and the Moon. The Earth's shadow can be seen crossing the Moon. The Moon looks a lot darker and reddish but it does not disappear completely.

LIGHT PILLARS

These columns of light stretch up or down from sources of light including the Sun, Moon or even streetlamps. They are caused by the light bouncing off ice crystals in the air.

RARE CLOUDS

Noctilucent, or night-shining, clouds are Earth's highest clouds. They form on ice crystals and dust near the edge of space. They appear after sunset and look very alien with their ripples of bright blue across the sky.

UNEXPECTED INGREDIENTS

TREES ⟶ PAPER

Most of the paper we use is made from trees. The wood is chopped up and then soaked and ground into a pulp. This is treated with chemicals and dyes before being pressed and dried into sheets of paper. The sheets are rolled up and cut to size.

SAND ⟶ GLASS

Sand is mixed with other ingredients, such as soda ash and limestone, and then heated to a very high temperature. This makes a liquid that can be moulded or blown into anything from windowpanes to beautiful glass ornaments.

OIL ⟶ MAKE-UP

Crude oil is a fossil fuel that has many uses. It is made into gas, diesel and fuel for airplanes. Chemicals from processing the oil are also used in the making of many beauty products such as skin creams and make-up.

SEAWEED ⟶ TOOTHPASTE

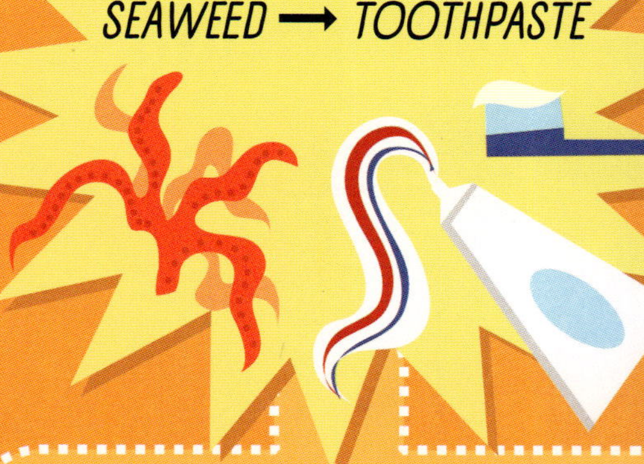

TREE LIQUID ⟶ TIRES

The liquid from rubber trees is called latex. The trees are cut and the milky-white latex flows into small buckets. It can be made into all kinds of useful things like tires, hoses, rubber bands, gloves and ducks for bath time!

You need to be able to squeeze your toothpaste out of its tube. Seaweed contains something called carrageenan that is added to the paste to make it the right thickness. Seaweed extracts can also be added to ice-cream to make it smooth and stop ice crystals from forming.

WORD TO KNOW

MANUFACTURE

comes from two Latin words: manus = hand, facere = to make. Most manufacturing is done in factories these days!

Diamonds are extremely hard and do not melt easily. This means they can be used as drill-heads for powering through rocks, bricks and concrete, for example on oil rigs.

Silk is a beautiful fabric woven from an unusual thread that comes from the cocoons of silkworms. These are not worms at all but the caterpillars of the silk moth. They munch away on mulberry leaves before spinning their cocoons of fine thread.

Next time you pop a red sweet into your mouth think about how it got its red color. Red food dyes, called cochineal and carmine, are made out of ground-up insects. They are added to many pink or red-colored foods and cosmetics.

SILVER → BANDAGES

Silver is very good at fighting off bacteria that cause infection. Many medical instruments are made using silver. Bandages with just a small amount of silver in them can help wounds to heal more quickly.

WHIZZY STUFF IN THE GALAXIES

TELESCOPES IN ORBIT

These can see further into space than telescopes on the ground. They send back amazing images of stars, planets and galaxies. The Hubble Space Telescope has been doing this since 1990. The largest space telescope is the James Webb Space Telescope which was launched in 2021.

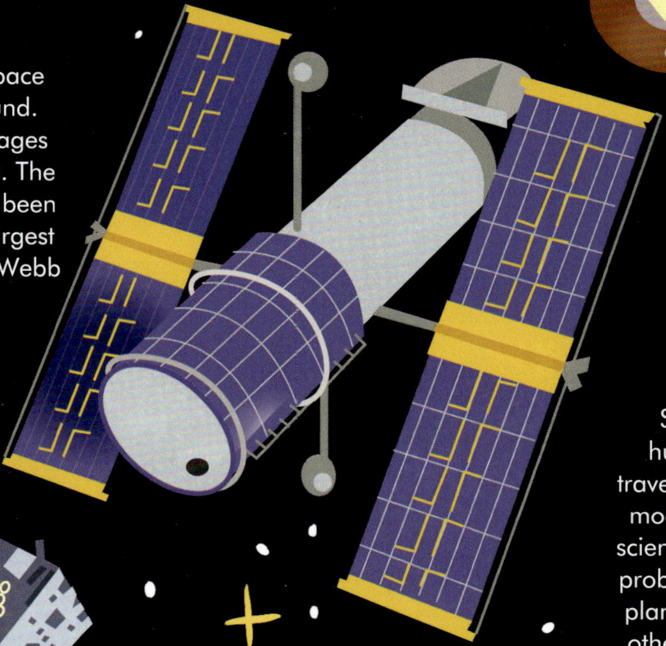

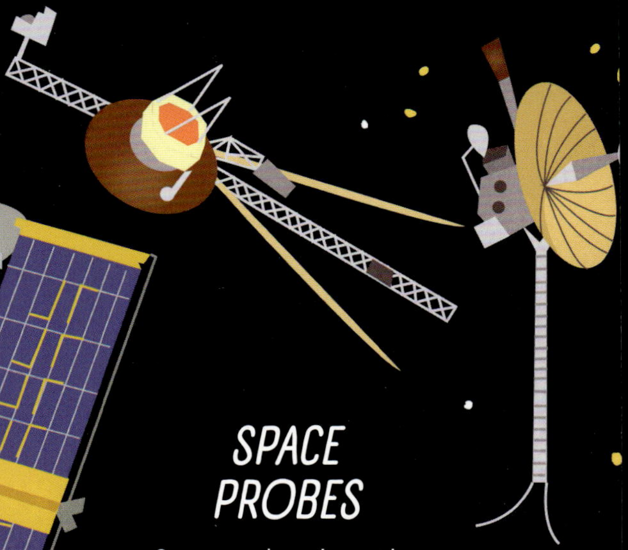

SPACE PROBES

Space probes do not have humans on board. They can travel for years to other planets or moons to collect and send back scientific information. Some space probes go into orbit around other planets, some land on them and others leave our Solar System to explore far into space.

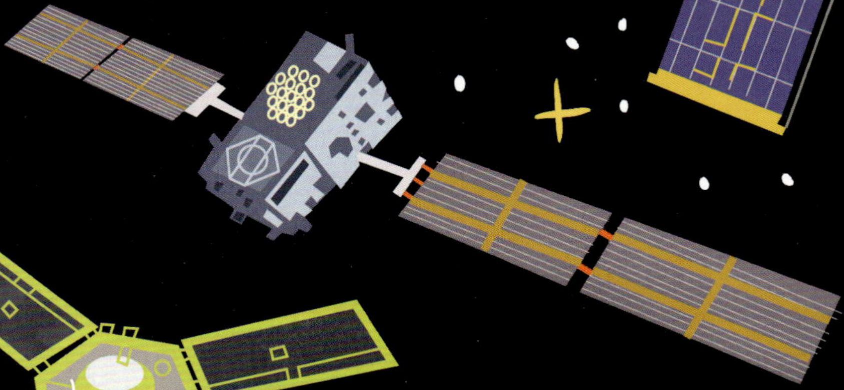

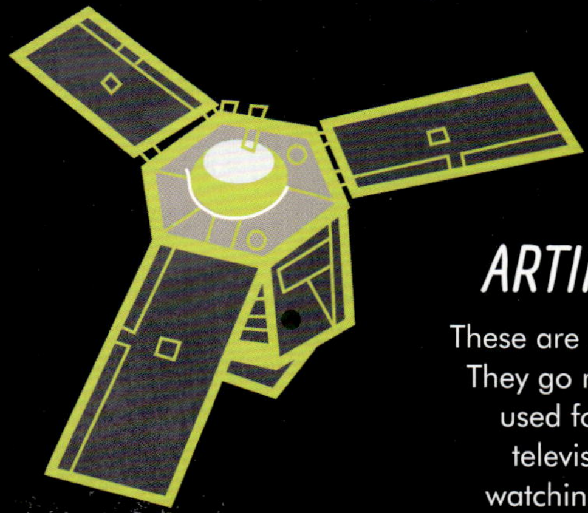

ARTIFICIAL SATELLITES

These are launched into space by rockets. They go round (orbit) the Earth and are used for communications, sending television and phone signals, for watching the weather, for helping us navigate the planet and for spying!

METEORS

There are little chunks of rock in space called meteoroids. When they reach the Earth's atmosphere they get really hot and burn up, looking like amazing fireworks streaking across the sky. These are called meteors or, sometimes, shooting stars.

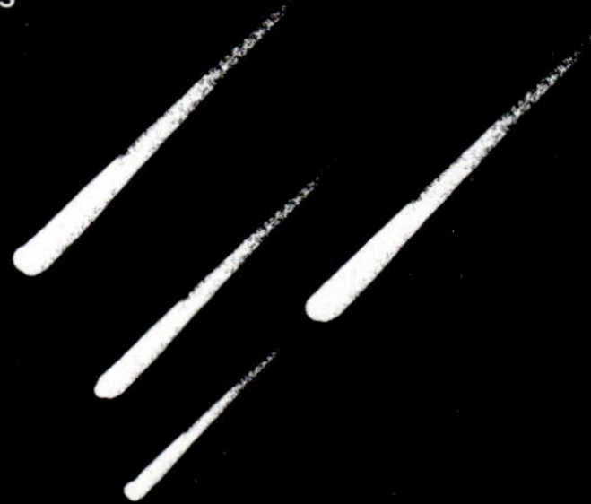

METEORITE

When a meteor hits the Earth it is called a meteorite. Some of them have made huge holes, or craters, in the ground. In Arizona, USA there is a massive one over 1 kilometer wide.

WORD TO KNOW

CELESTIAL

describes things in the sky or outer space. Planets and stars are celestial bodies.

NEBULAE

Nebulae are enormous gas clouds in space where stars are born. Stars are huge balls of burning gas. As the stars get bigger, the nebulae begin to glow. The nearest star to Earth is the Sun.

WHITE DWARF

Some red giants slowly shrink and become stars that are called white dwarfs.

RED GIANT

Stars burn for billions of years, but then they begin to run out of gas. They then change from white to red, grow bigger and become red giants.

COMETS

These are great big dirty ice balls that can be several miles across. If they come close to the Sun the ice in them melts and creates a tail of dust and gas. Halley's Comet can be seen from Earth every 75–76 years. Its next visit will be 2061.

BLACK HOLE

This may form after a star has exploded. It is a very tight ball of gas that has such a huge pull of gravity that it even sucks light into it.

SUPERNOVA

Other red giants get bigger and bigger until there is gigantic explosion called a supernova.

TECHNOLOGY IN THE CITY

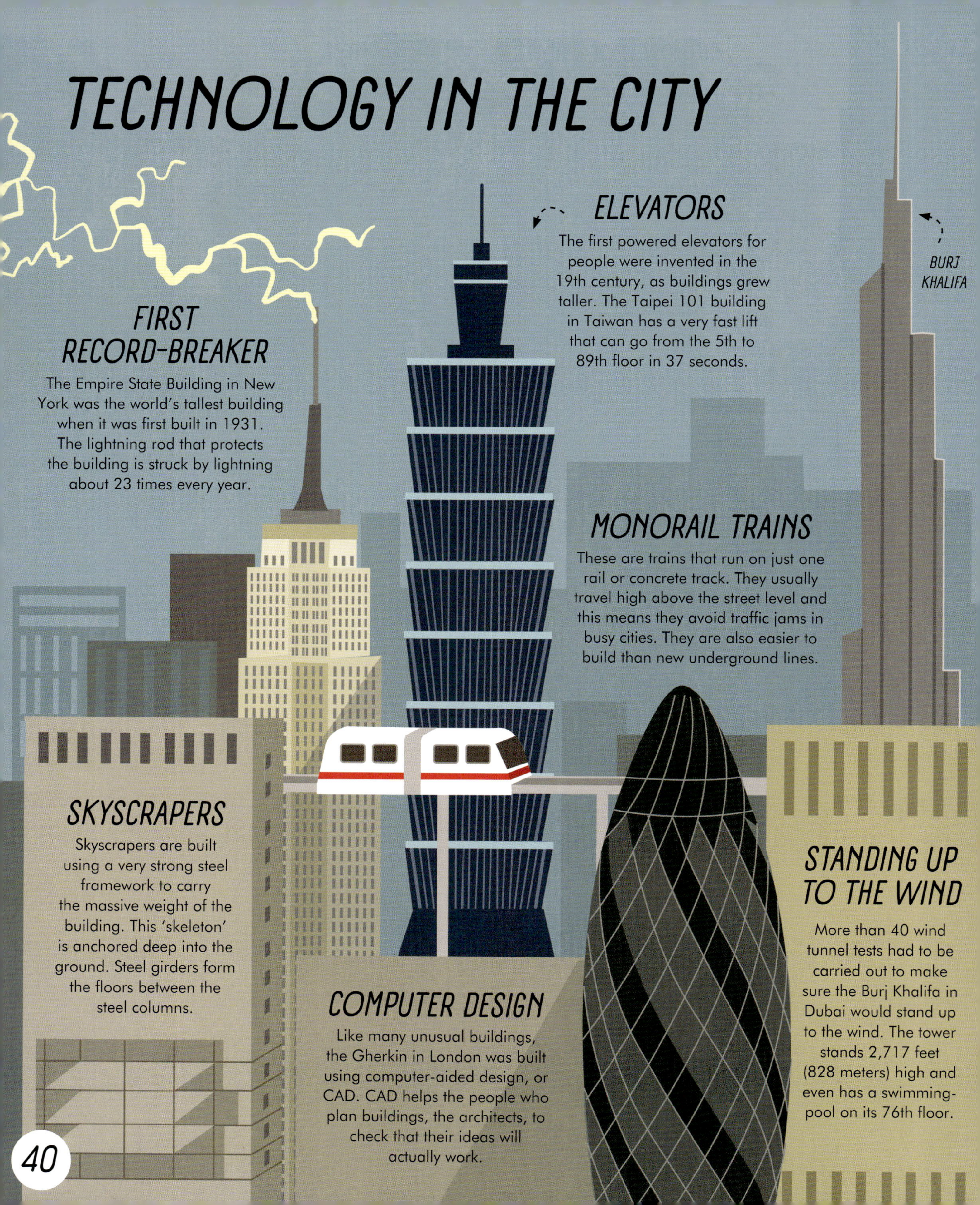

FIRST RECORD-BREAKER

The Empire State Building in New York was the world's tallest building when it was first built in 1931. The lightning rod that protects the building is struck by lightning about 23 times every year.

ELEVATORS

The first powered elevators for people were invented in the 19th century, as buildings grew taller. The Taipei 101 building in Taiwan has a very fast lift that can go from the 5th to 89th floor in 37 seconds.

BURJ KHALIFA

MONORAIL TRAINS

These are trains that run on just one rail or concrete track. They usually travel high above the street level and this means they avoid traffic jams in busy cities. They are also easier to build than new underground lines.

SKYSCRAPERS

Skyscrapers are built using a very strong steel framework to carry the massive weight of the building. This 'skeleton' is anchored deep into the ground. Steel girders form the floors between the steel columns.

COMPUTER DESIGN

Like many unusual buildings, the Gherkin in London was built using computer-aided design, or CAD. CAD helps the people who plan buildings, the architects, to check that their ideas will actually work.

STANDING UP TO THE WIND

More than 40 wind tunnel tests had to be carried out to make sure the Burj Khalifa in Dubai would stand up to the wind. The tower stands 2,717 feet (828 meters) high and even has a swimming-pool on its 76th floor.

INFRASTRUCTURE

describes the system of roads, buildings, power and communications that make a city work.

SELF-CLEANING GLASS

Many modern skyscrapers are built with windows made from self-cleaning glass. The glass has a special coating on it to prevent dirt from sticking to it

ESCALATORS

These moving staircases transport people up and down in shopping malls, stations and other large buildings. In the Moscow Metro there is one escalator that is so long you cannot see the top when you are at the bottom. It takes three minutes, or long enough to boil an egg, to ride it.

CLEVER LIGHTS

Many cities now use a kind of light bulb called an LED in streetlights. They do not use much energy and last for a long time. Modern lights can also be set up so that they get brighter when people and traffic are there, and dimmer if the street is empty.

SMART CITIES

Streetlamps can also have other gadgets called sensors attached to them. These can take in information about all sorts of things like the weather, pollution and noise.

UNDERGROUND TRAINS

The first underground train system opened in London in 1863 with steam trains. Technology has, of course, improved since then and some metro systems in the world now even use trains without drivers.

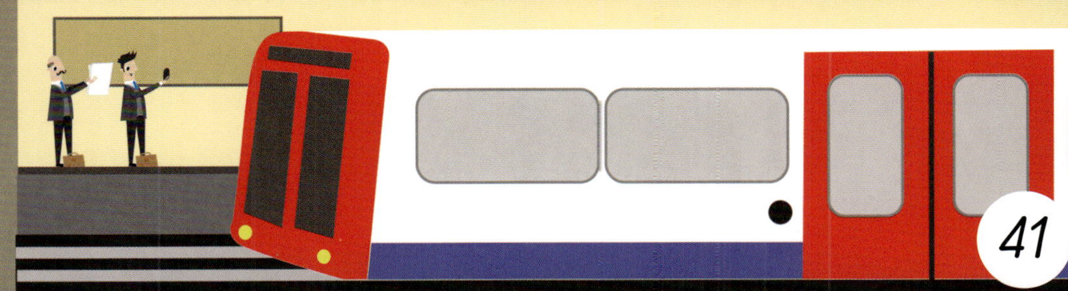

HOW AIRPORTS WORK

FIREFIGHTERS

Airports have their own special firefighters on hand. Some fire engines have hoses with nozzles that can break through the side of an aircraft. They are called 'snozzles'!

CHECKING-IN AND BOARDING

The people we show our tickets to are called passenger handling agents or passenger service agents. They weigh and label our luggage and also check our boarding passes just before we get on the plane.

AIRPORT VETS

Animals have to travel in special crates and are usually put in the cargo hold. Airports have trained animal handlers and vets to look after them.

WORD TO KNOW

AERODROME

is a landing area for planes that is not as large as an airport. An aerodrome is mainly used by smaller aircraft.

CUSTOMS OFFICERS

These officers check that passengers are not bringing anything forbidden, or illegal, into a country. They search luggage and use sniffer dogs to help them.

AIRFIELD OPERATIONS

The people working on the airfield make sure that the runways are safe. They check for holes, clear ice and snow and scare birds away with loud noises.

AIR TRAFFIC CONTROL

Air traffic controllers sit in a control tower and instruct pilots on their speed, height and route. They work 24 hours a day and must not make a mistake.

GROUND SERVICES

The ground crew handles mountains of suitcases every day, getting them transported on to and off planes. They also direct, or marshal, the planes on and off the stands where they are parked.

IMMIGRATION OFFICERS

Every international airport has immigration officers to check passengers' passports. They can ask why they are travelling to a country and must look out for any suspicious behavior.

SECURITY

Airport security officers x-ray baggage to make sure it does not contain anything dangerous like knives, guns or bombs. They also ask people to go through special metal-detecting gates.

PILOTS AND CABIN CREW

There are usually two pilots on a plane, a captain and a first officer. The flight attendants, or cabin crew, look after the passengers.

THE PAINTER'S TOOLKIT

CAVE PAINTERS

No one really knows why prehistoric humans made cave paintings. They made paints out of red, yellow, black and brown rocks and earth. They probably used hollowed-out bones to blow the paint on the walls, sometimes using their own hands as a kind of stencil.

WATERCOLORS AND GOUACHE

Watercolors are transparent, water-based paints in tubes or solid blocks called 'pans'. They are ideal for painting using layers of color. Gouache is similar, but chalk is added to the pigments to make it opaque rather than transparent.

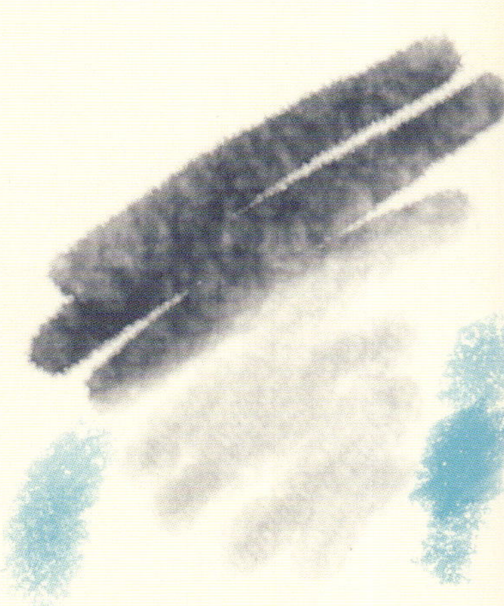

PAINTING WITH EGGS

Before oil paints, artists used a kind of fast-drying paint called egg tempera. It was made from mixing ground-up colors, or pigments, with egg yolk. It had to be made freshly each time it was needed.

PORTABLE KIT

The first oil paints had to be mixed each time you needed them. In the 1840s, oils in metal tubes were invented. With folding easels and small canvases this meant that painters could paint wherever they liked, and especially outside in the countryside.

CANVAS AND OTHER SURFACES

A canvas is made from a rough cotton or linen cloth, usually stretched across a wooden frame. Painters also paint on walls, wood, paper and sometimes metal, glass, slate or even themselves!

OIL PAINTS

By the 1500s artists were using paints made by mixing colors with linseed or walnut oil. Oil paint dries slowly and is ideal for painting on canvas. It can be used for delicate shading or wonderful gloopy, thick effects.

BRUSHES AND PALETTE KNIVES

Brushes are made from all kinds of natural animal or man-made hair. Bristly brushes are best for oil paints, but fine, soft brushes are needed for watercolors. A palette knife is used for mixing paint but it can also be good for putting oil paints on to a canvas.

WORD TO KNOW

CHIAROSCURO

is an Italian word used to describe the contrasting effects of light and shade in a painting.

ART ON A SCREEN

Modern technology means that some artists use a tablet computer to create a painting. It is easy to make changes and alter the colors as they go along.

NOT PAINT!

Some modern artists, like Picasso, make paintings using all kinds of other materials like bits of newspaper, catalogues, old string and rope. An artist called Anselm Kiefer uses straw, mud and even diamonds with paint to create an artwork.

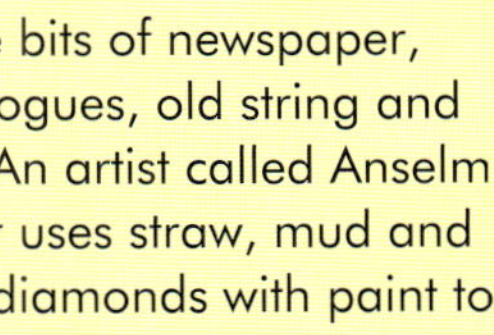

MEGA MACHINES

SUPERTANKERS

These are the largest ships in the world. They carry liquid cargo like oil across the oceans. They are so huge that it can take them up to 6 miles (10 kilometers) to stop!

CRUISE LINERS

The largest cruise liners are like small floating towns for several thousand holidaymakers. They have restaurants, shops, cinemas, theatres, tennis courts, spas and swimming-pools.

BENDY BUSES

These are like two buses stuck together. Only one driver is needed and they can carry more people around crowded cities and towns.

ARTICULATED LORRIES

The biggest lorries have a separate engine and cab for the driver. This is called a tractor. All kinds of trailers for carrying loads can be attached at the back. Some of them are enormous.

CARGO CRANES

Huge metal boxes, or containers, are used to transport all sorts of goods all over the world. Massive cranes lift them on and off gigantic container ships.

TOWER CRANES

These giants are essential for lifting the heavy materials used to build skyscrapers. The crane operator sits in a little cabin high up above the ground.

GIANT BORING MACHINES

These are used to make tunnels for new train lines or routes under rivers or through mountains. Some of these mighty machines even have their own toilet and kitchen for the crew.

GIANT MIXERS

Loads of concrete is needed on building sites. The mixers fetch sand, cement and gravel from a factory. The drum keeps turning as they drive along to mix the concrete and stop it from going hard.

EXCAVATORS

These powerful mega-diggers are used to excavate trenches and holes, and to clear rubble and earth. The driver sits in a cab that can turn a complete circle.

WORD TO KNOW

MECHANICAL

describes the way that engines and machines work.

WRITING AROUND THE WORLD

ALPHABETS

An alphabet is a way of writing down what we say (our language), using letters for each sound. The word 'alphabet' comes from the first two letters of the ancient Greek alphabet 'alpha' (=a) and 'beta' (=b).

PHOENICIAN ALPHABET

About 3,000 years ago, the Phoenicians who lived around the Mediterranean Sea created an alphabet with 22 letters. It was much easier to use than some other early forms of writing. The Greek, Roman, Arabic and Hebrew alphabets all developed from this.

ROMAN WRITING

The Romans used an alphabet similar to the ancient Greek one. As they marched across Europe they brought it with them. In Britain, France, Italy, Spain, Portugal and many other countries it is still used today.

A B C D E F
G H I K L M
N O P Q R S
T V X Y Z

ANCIENT GREEK

The ancient Greeks improved the Phoenician alphabet by adding letters for vowel sounds (a, e, i, o, u). It made everything much easier to understand. However, they still did not have any commas or full stops and there were no gaps between any of the words!

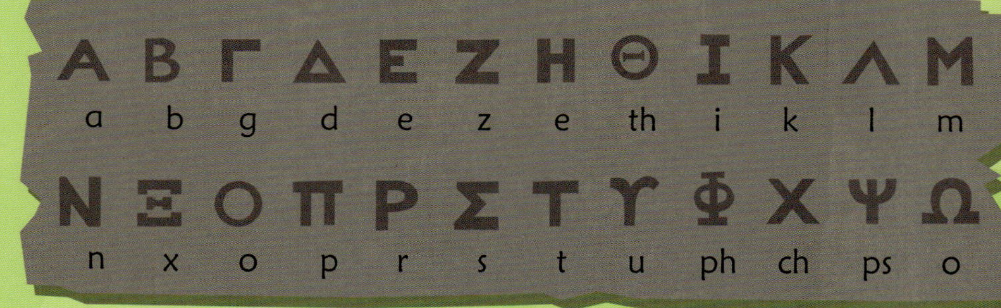

English	Hello
French	Bonjour
Spanish	¡Hola!
Italian	Ciao
Portuguese	Olá

Hello
marhaba
مرحبا

ARABIC

Arabic is written and read from right to left across the page. It is used all over the Arab world in countries such as Algeria, Egypt, Saudi Arabia and Iraq.

WORD TO KNOW

MANUSCRIPT

comes from the Latin 'manus' (hand) and 'scriptum' (writing). A manuscript was a book written by hand before the invention of printing.

Hello
zdravstvuj
здравствуй

CYRILLIC ALPHABET

This alphabet grew out of the Greek alphabet. It is used by people in countries like Russia, Bulgaria and Serbia to write down their languages.

Hello
shalom
שלום

HEBREW

Like Arabic, Hebrew is written and read from right to left. It is the language used in Israel and by Jewish people all over the world.

Hello
namastē
नमस्ते

DEVANAGARI ALPHABET

This is the main alphabet of northern India and is used to write down Hindi and other Indian languages. It is also sometimes called the Nagari alphabet.

Hello
ni hao
你好

CHINESE CHARACTERS

Chinese is one of the oldest kinds of writing that is still used by people today. It uses characters rather than letters of an alphabet. These characters stand for things or ideas. Chinese children have to learn thousands of these characters at school.

Hello
annyeonghaseyo
안녕하세요

KOREAN WRITING

Korean is written down using characters for each syllable in a word. It is said that King Sejong of Korea invented this writing system in the fifteenth century. It is called Hangul, a word with two syllables written like this:

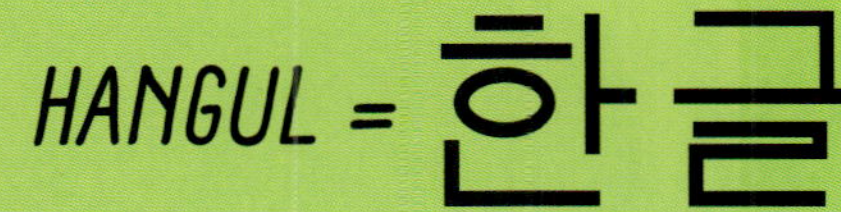

WORDS TO KNOW

AERODROME is a landing area for planes that is not as large as an airport. It is mainly used by smaller aircraft.

AERONAUTICS is the science of designing and building aircraft.

ARBOREAL means 'living up in trees'. It is very handy to be an arboreal creature if you are in a rainforest.

ARCHAEOLOGIST is someone who looks at ancient objects and buildings to find out how people lived in the past. They are like history detectives.

BIOLUMINESCENCE is light made by living organisms to attract attention, frighten enemies, use as a disguise, or to find prey in the dark.

CELESTIAL describes things in the sky or outer space, like stars and planets.

CENTRIPETAL is the name given to the force that stops you falling out of your seat on a roller coaster. Centripetal force keeps you pressed into your chair when looping the loop.

CETACEAN is the word for a sea mammal that has to come up to the surface to breathe. Cetology is the study of whales, dolphins and porpoises.

CHIAROSCURO is an Italian word used to describe the contrasting effects of light and shade in a painting.

CIRCUMNAVIGATE means to travel all the way around something. Many explorers have circumnavigated the world.

CREPUSCULE means the time of day just after sunset.

FORTIFICATION means a wall or other strong structure built to defend a place against attack.

INFRASTRUCTURE is the system of roads, buildings, power and communications that make a city work.

MANUFACTURE means to make things, usually using machinery in a factory.

MANUSCRIPT is a book, or document, written by hand before the invention of printing.

MECHANICAL describes the way that engines and machines work.

MEGAHERBIVORES are huge, plant-eating creatures like the largest of the dinosaurs.

MICROGRAVITY means that even heavy things seem not to weigh anything, and people and objects can float around. There is only a small ('micro') amount of gravity in a space station.

MIMICRY is when a creature pretends to be something else to protect itself or to find prey.

NON-RENEWABLE describes energy that comes from sources that will run out. We cannot make any more of them.

RENEWABLE describes energy that comes from things that do not run out, like the Sun or the sea.

TROGLODYTE means someone who lives in a cave.

VELOCITY means the speed and direction of an object or living creature.

The WONDERFUL WORLD in FIGURES

EARTH IN SPACE

There are billions of stars in the Universe. Stars look small, but they are really huge balls of burning gas. Some stars also have massive balls of rock, or planets, circling round them. Planet Earth orbits a star called the Sun. Other planets also orbit the Sun to make a space neighborhood that we call the Solar System.

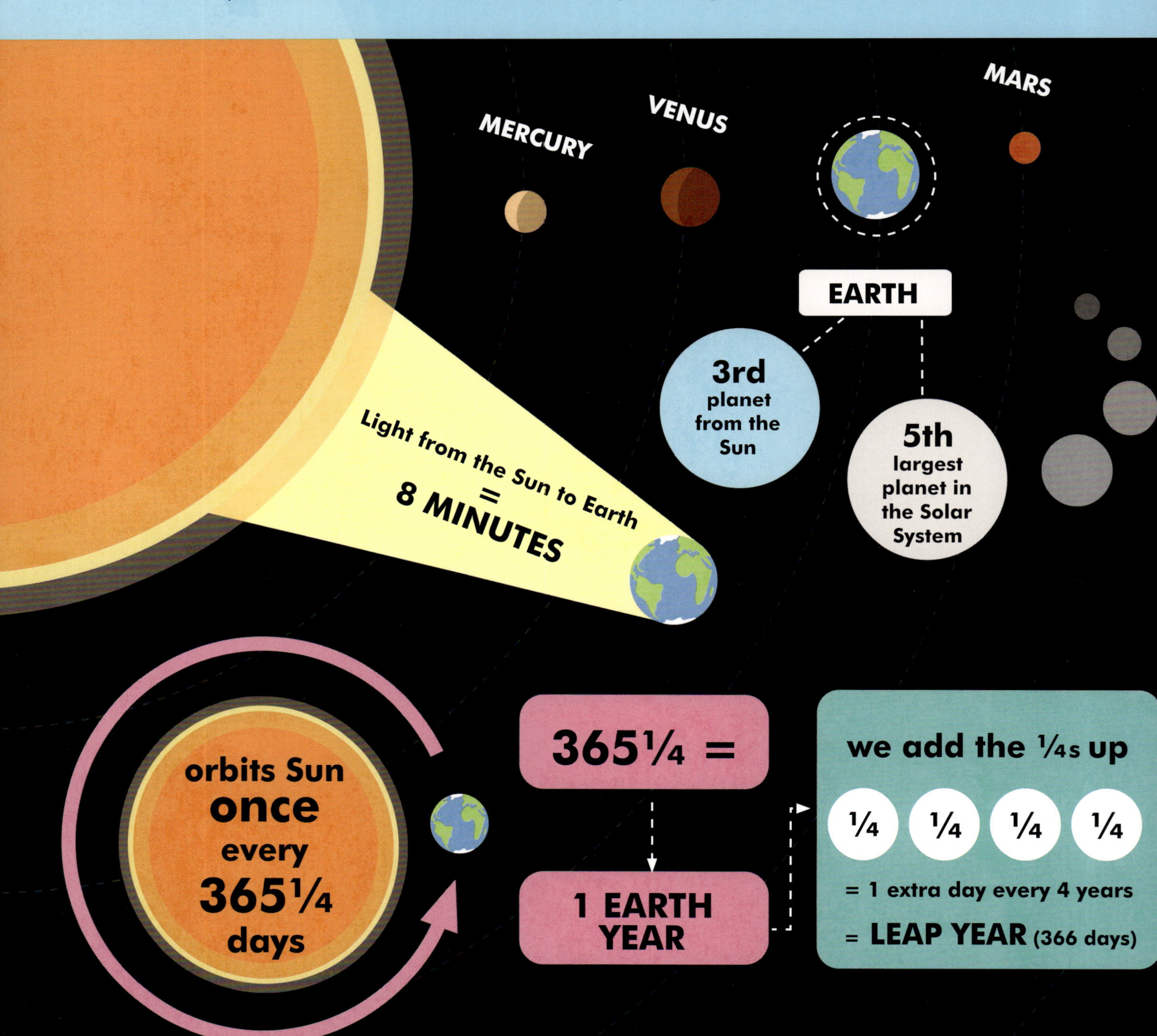

An **ASTRONOMER** investigates stars, planets and galaxies. Astronomy is the study of everything in the Universe.

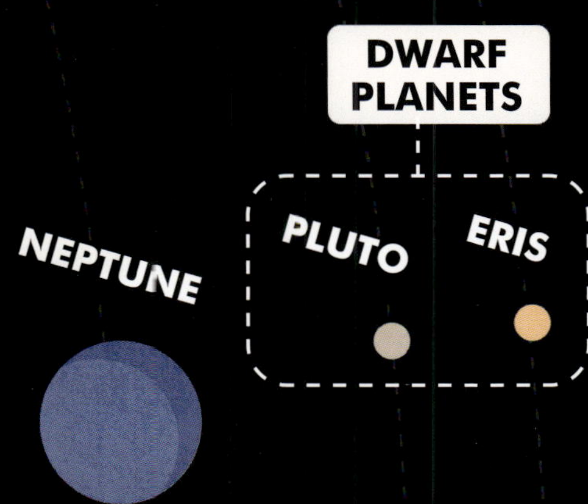

Earth has 1 moon

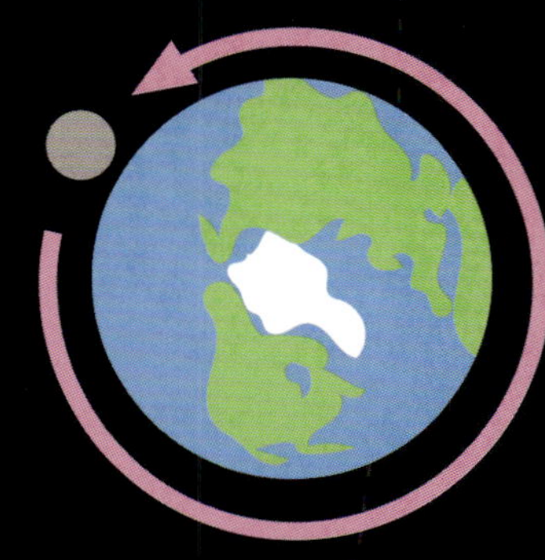

The Moon is getting further away from Earth by about as much as your fingernails grow each year.

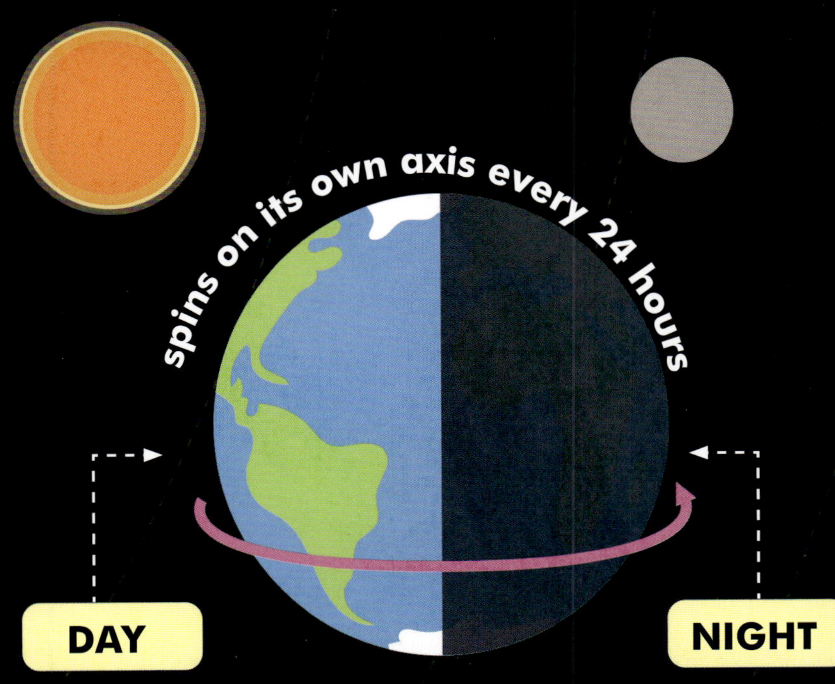

Planet Earth is not a perfect round sphere. It's really the shape of a slightly squashed ball. It is a little flatter at the top and the bottom.

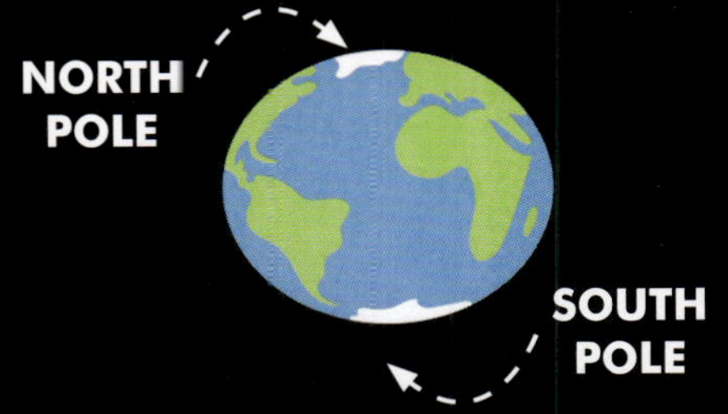

THE ATMOSPHERE

There is a giant blanket of air around Planet Earth. It is called the atmosphere and it is made of different layers. The layer nearest Earth is really important as it keeps us warm and gives us oxygen to breathe. It is also where our weather happens.

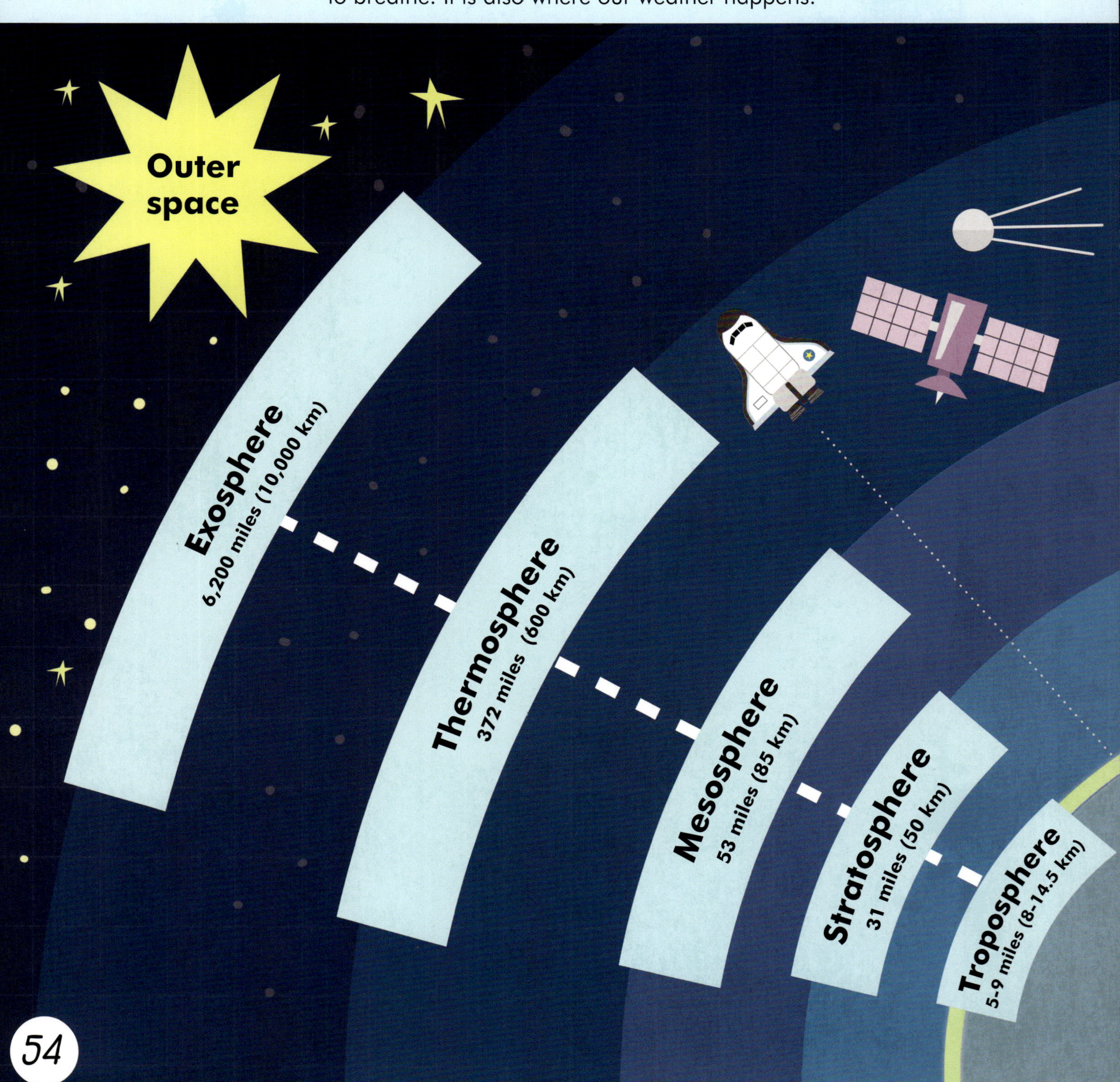

WORKING ON THE PLANET
METEOROLOGISTS look at the atmosphere to study the weather and our climate. They try to predict the weather and how it will affect our planet.
International Space Station 250 miles (402 km)
60 mph (100 kph)
Highest parachute jump 25.7 miles (41.4 km)
4 days and nights
There is a special gas in the Stratosphere called ozone. The ozone is a bit like a massive dollop of sunscreen as it protects our planet from too much sun!
Mount Everest 29,029 feet (8,848 m)

JOURNEY TO THE CENTER OF THE EARTH

The Earth under our feet is like a giant onion with four layers. No one has ever travelled to the center of the planet, but scientists think that they know what might be in each layer. They also think that the very center of the Earth is actually a solid ball of metal.

CRUST

about **19 miles (30 km) thick** on land and about **3 miles (5 km) thick** at the bottom of the ocean

MANTLE

1,800 miles (2,900 km) thick

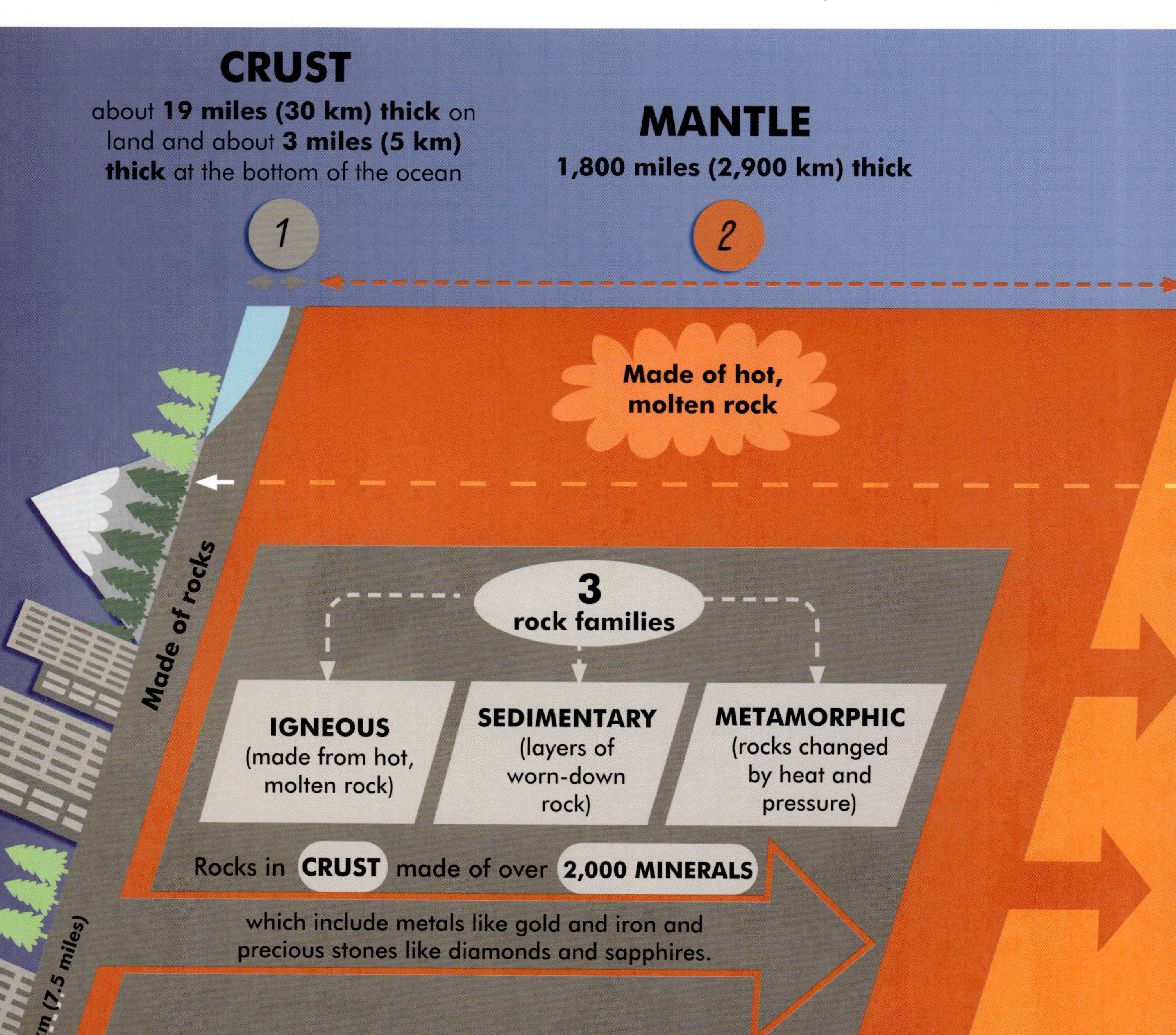

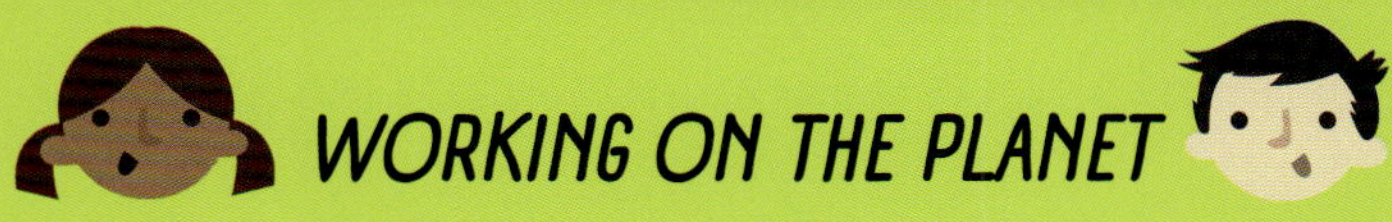

GEOLOGISTS study the solid surface of our planet. They investigate how our planet was first made by looking at the rocks in and on it.

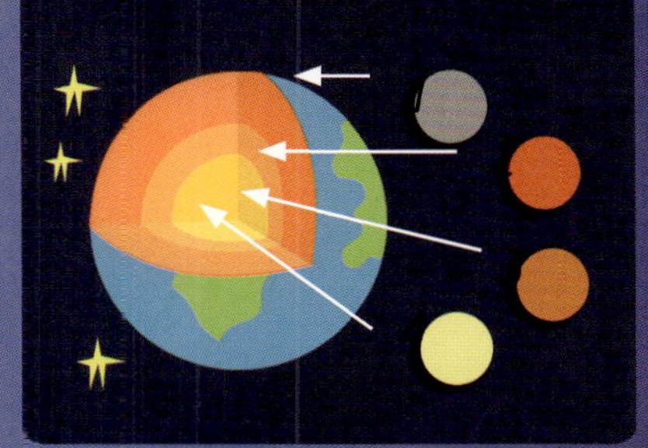

HOTTEST PART

of core is as hot as the Sun 10,800°F (6,000°C)

OUTER CORE

1,367 miles (2,200 km) thick

3

INNER CORE

radius 758 miles (1,220 km)

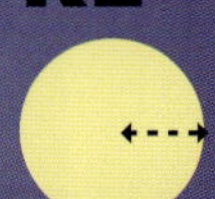

4

Made of liquid metal

Made of solid metal

It would take me a month at **6 mph (10 kph)...**

... to get to the center of the Earth!

SO HOT and under **SO MUCH PRESSURE** = **LIQUID METAL GOES SOLID**

The deepest hole ever drilled is in Russia and is called the Kola Superdeep Borehole. It took **20 years** to reach a depth of

7.5 miles
12 km

before the drill got too hot to carry on!

Inner core rotates (turns) more quickly than the rest of the Earth's layers.

But it takes **1,000** years to do one extra rotation!

MOVING PLATES

The ground you walk on is not as solid as you might think. The surface of the Earth is like a massive jigsaw of pieces or 'plates' that move. These plates are under the oceans and seas, too.

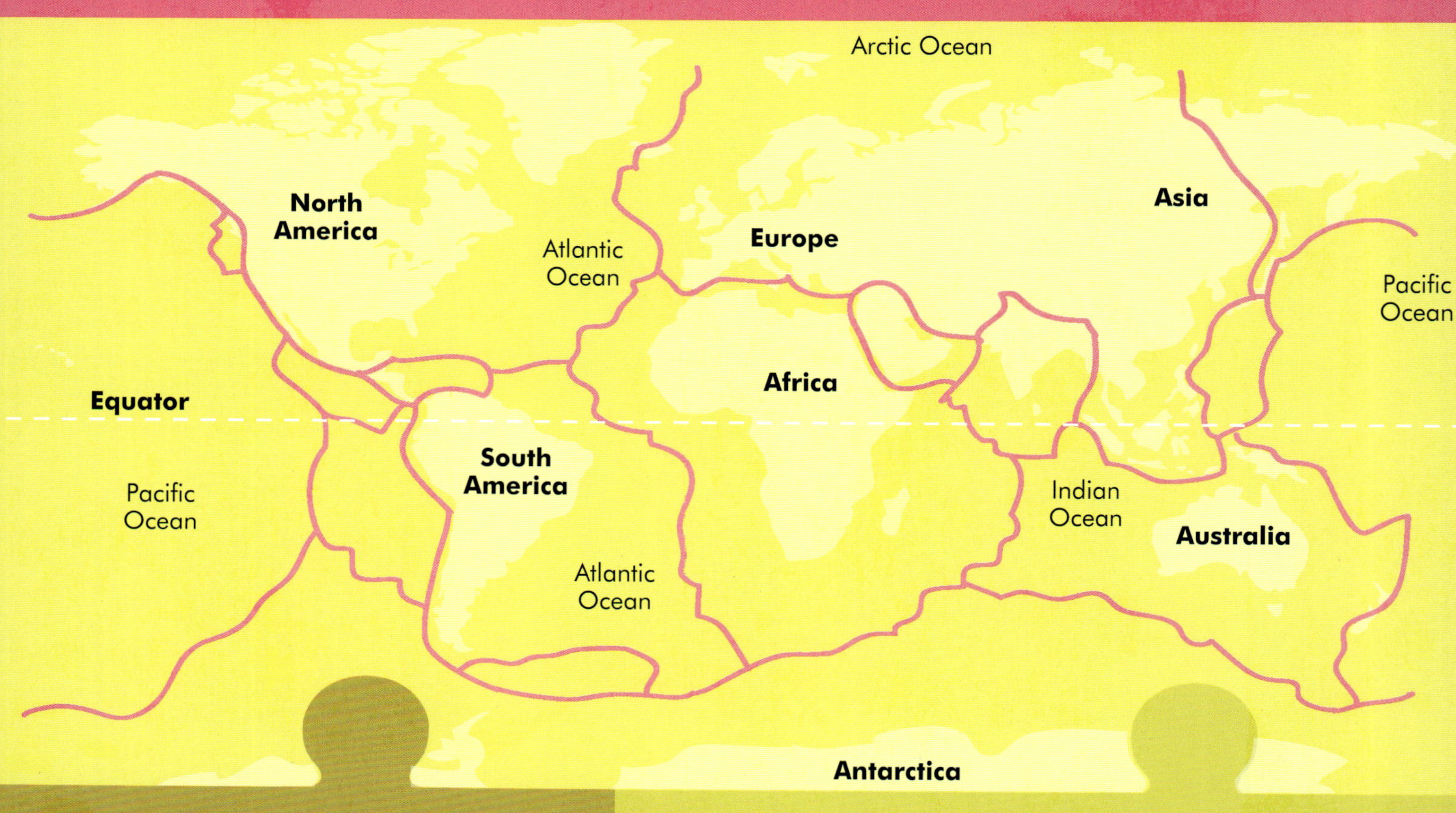

Scientific name for plates =

TECTONIC PLATES

Plates make the Earth's continents move from

½ inch (1 cm)

to 4 inches (10 cm) in a year.

Plates are **thinner** under oceans than on land.

SEISMOLOGISTS study earthquakes. They measure the shock waves caused by earthquakes and they try to predict when earthquakes will happen. This can save lives.

About **270 million** years ago the continents on our planet used to be one giant slab of land. Scientists call this mega-continent **Pangaea.**

Volcanoes

Most of the world's active volcanoes lie where

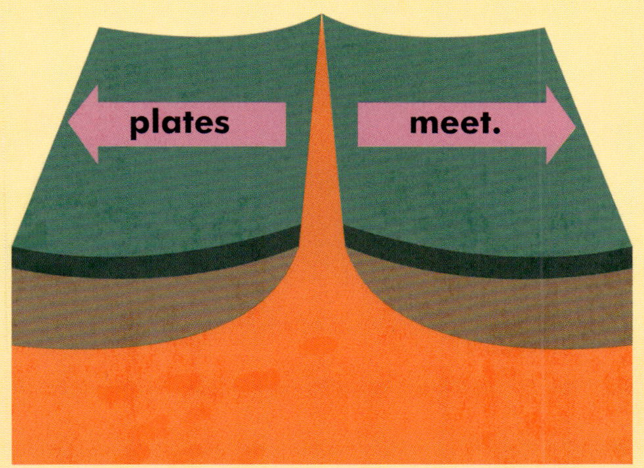

could **ERUPT** again!

Planet Earth has **1,900 ACTIVE** volcanoes.

Earthquakes

happen when plates slip against each other.

Tsunamis

big earthquakes under the ocean → gigantic, destructive waves

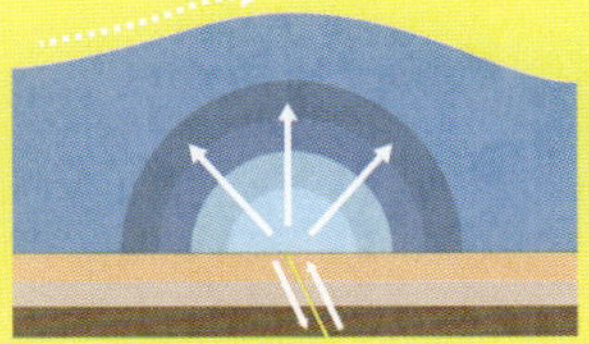

Earthquake

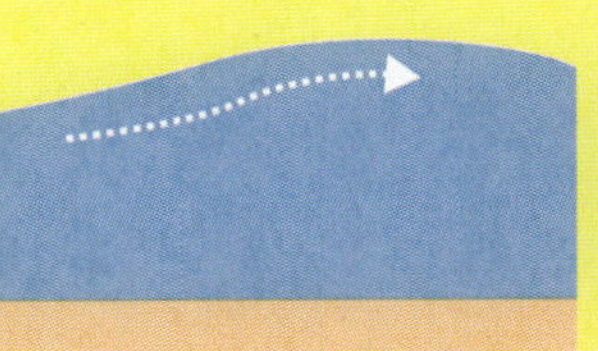

Shock wave

Tsunami

In 2004 a tsunami in the Indian Ocean killed over **230,000** people.

Speed of wave was as fast as a plane

500 mph (800 kph)

THE BLUE PLANET

Water covers more than two thirds of our beautiful planet. If you look at a map of the whole world you can see that the oceans are really all joined up. If you dip your toes in one ocean you are really dipping them into all the oceans on Earth!

5 MAIN OCEANS

How all the water in the oceans is divided up:

PACIFIC 50.1%

ATLANTIC 23.3%

INDIAN 19.8%

SOUTHERN OR ANTARCTIC 5.4%

ARCTIC 1.4%

But you would not want to drink this water. It's salty!

Pacific covers ONE THIRD of Earth's surface.

It is 3 x BIGGER than the BIGGEST CONTINENT...

ASIA.

An **OCEANOGRAPHER** explores the oceans from the depths of the sea floor to the surface and everything in between!

Waves are very powerful. The power of a wave crashing on to a beach is **30** times more powerful than the pressure of a human foot. This is how waves can smash rocks into sand!

Pacific Ocean contains

DEEPEST PLACE ON EARTH

Mariana Trench =
36,201 feet
(11,034 m)

That's over
6.8 miles
(11 km)
down!

The highest mountain on Earth would fit in it!

Mount Everest =
29,029 feet
(8,848 m)

0 m
1,000 m
2,000 m
3,000 m
4,000 m
5,000 m
6,000 m
7,000 m
8,000 m
9,000 m
10,000 m
11,000 m

Atlantic covers over **ONE FIFTH** of Earth's surface.

Indian is the **WARMEST** ocean.

Southern is around **SOUTH POLE. STRONGEST WINDS** on Earth.

Arctic is around **NORTH POLE. FROZEN** for most of the year.

THE BREATHING PLANET

Humans and other animals need a gas called oxygen to breathe. Oxygen in the Earth's atmosphere is made by plants and trees on land, and by tiny plants in the oceans. We need all these plants to make sure we have enough oxygen to stay alive!

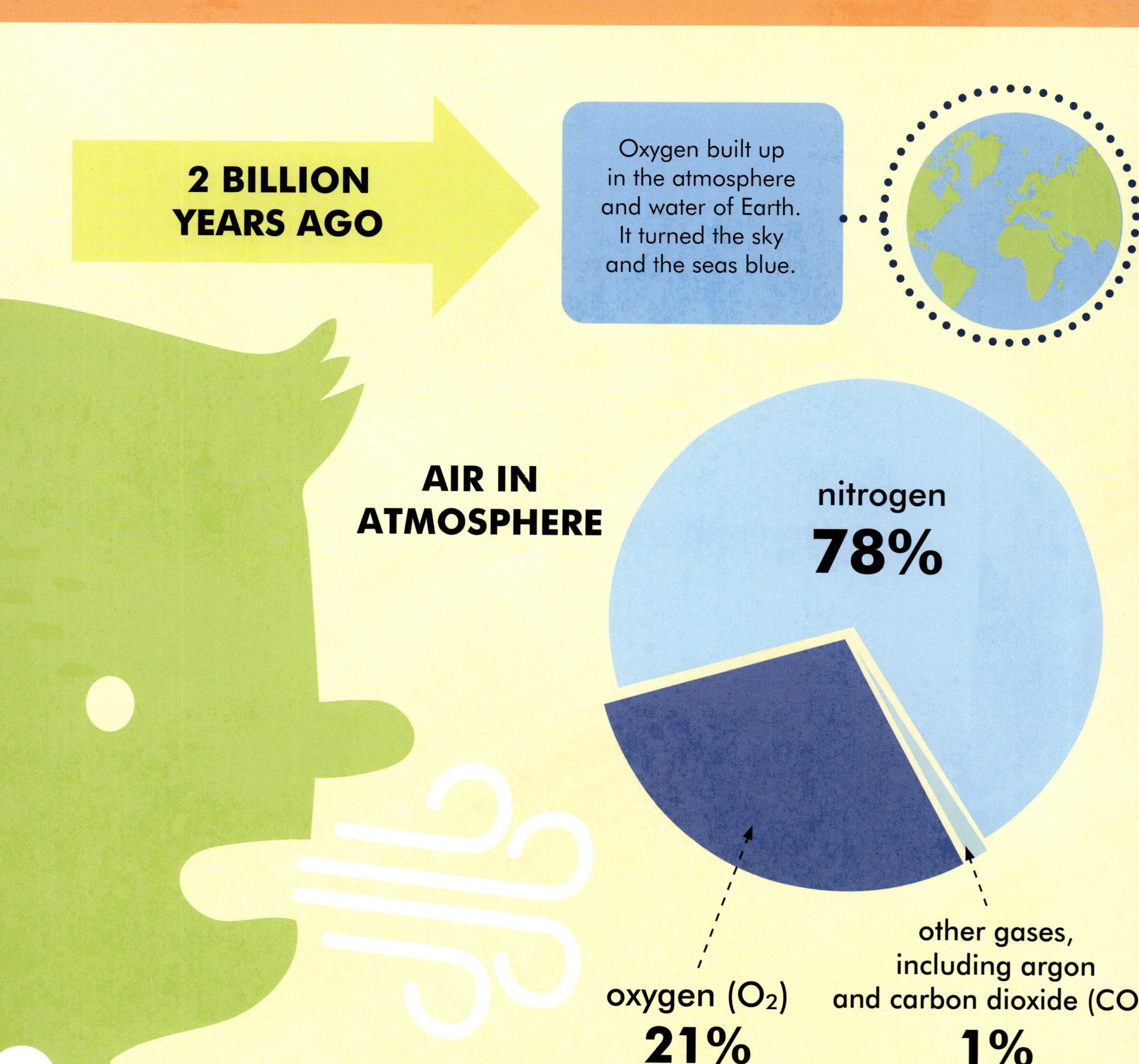

BOTANISTS are scientists who study everything to do with plants. The more we know about plant life, the better we can protect it.

The higher up the atmosphere you go

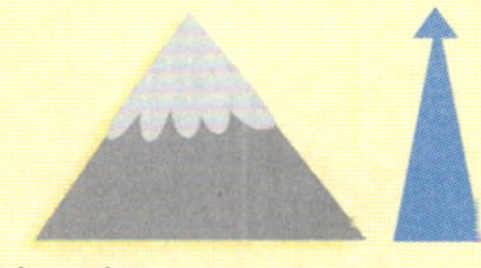

the thinner air gets.

It means there is less oxygen to breathe, too. That is why mountain climbers need to take extra oxygen with them!

LUNGS OF THE WORLD

Photosynthesis
Plants and trees use sunlight, water and carbon dioxide to make food for themselves.

TREES

HUMANS & ANIMALS

O_2

Trees breathe out oxygen. We breathe out carbon dioxide.

CO_2

1 PERSON **needs the oxygen from up to 8 TREES to breathe** **for 1 YEAR.**

Rainforests are so huge...

... they 'breathe in' LOTS of carbon dioxide

... and 'breathe out' LOTS of oxygen.

RESPIRATION is the scientific name for breathing.

INTO THE WOODS

Trees are amazing. Some of them can live for thousands of years. Forests cover about one third of the land on Earth. Different types, or species, of trees grow in a forest depending on where that forest is in the world.

Forests are 'carbon sinks'. They soak up the carbon dioxide that is causing dangerous changes to our planet's climate. This means it is very important to protect our forests as they look after us and our Earth home.

WORKING ON THE PLANET

FOREST RANGERS protect forests and all the trees and animals in them. They can spot any damage and take steps to repair forests if needed.

DESERTED EARTH

Deserts are the driest places on Earth. Deserts can be scorching hot, but did you know that deserts can be very cold, too? In fact, Antarctica and the Arctic are polar deserts!

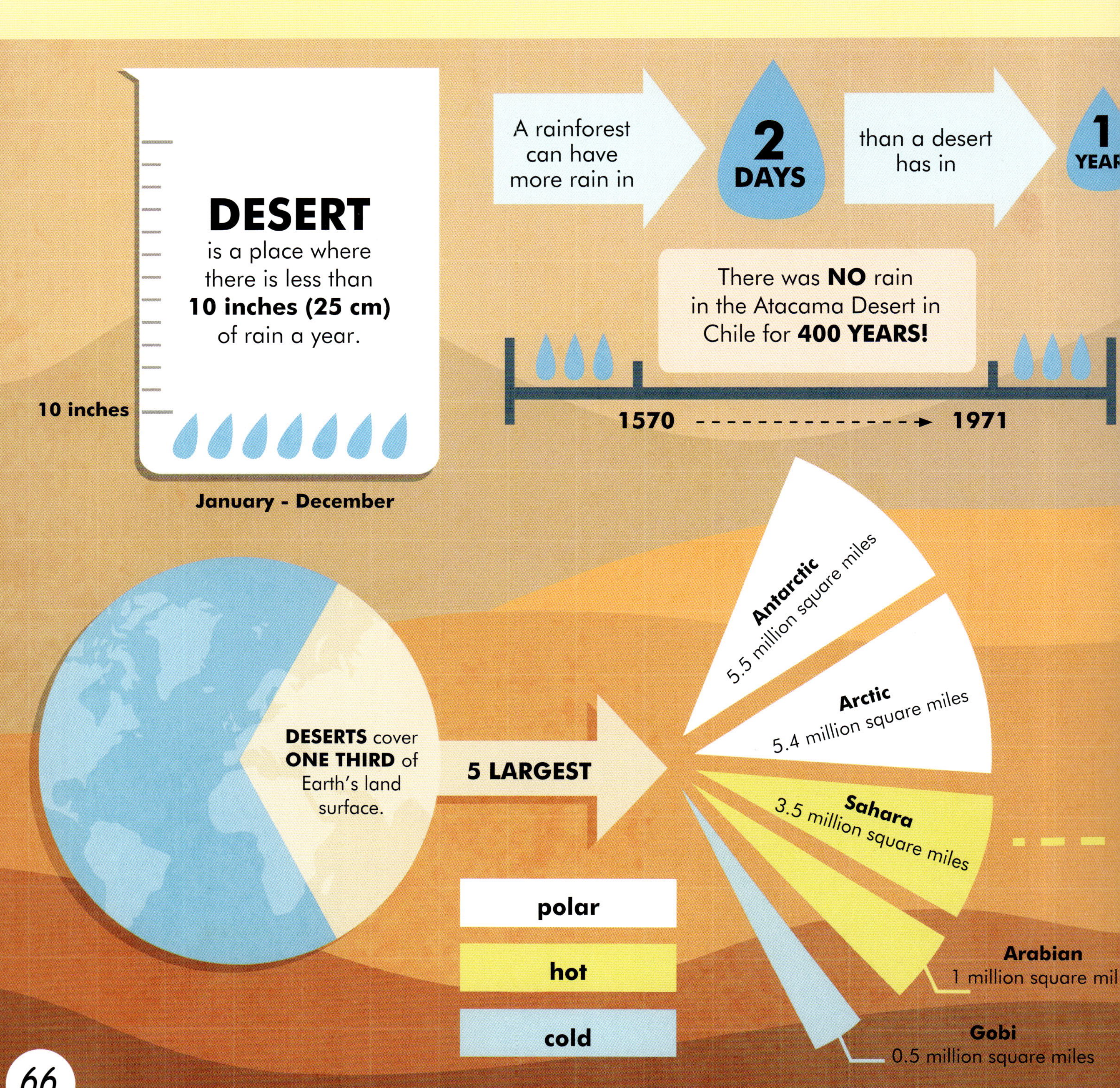

WORKING ON THE PLANET

An **ECOLOGIST** studies how environments, like deserts, affect the animals and plants living in them. The ecologist looks at the smallest forms of life as well as the bigger 'picture' of the environment.

The **Antarctic** and **Arctic** deserts are always cold, but even hot deserts can be cold at night. The boiling hot day temperatures can drop down to freezing.

(32°F)
0°C

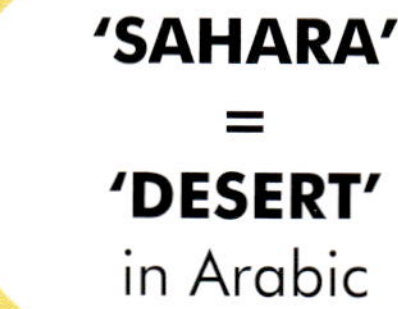

'SAHARA'
=
'DESERT'
in Arabic

The **Sahara** is bigger than the **USA** and getting **BIGGER** every day.

SANDSTORMS can **BLAST** the paint off a car!

Sahara is

30%

70%

gravel

HELLO PEOPLE!

Scientists think that there have been creatures like humans on the planet for two million years. But the first humans who were most like us are called *Homo sapiens*. This means 'wise man' in Latin. Once they began to explore the world there was no stopping them – or us!

Homo sapiens lived in Africa about **200,000** years ago.

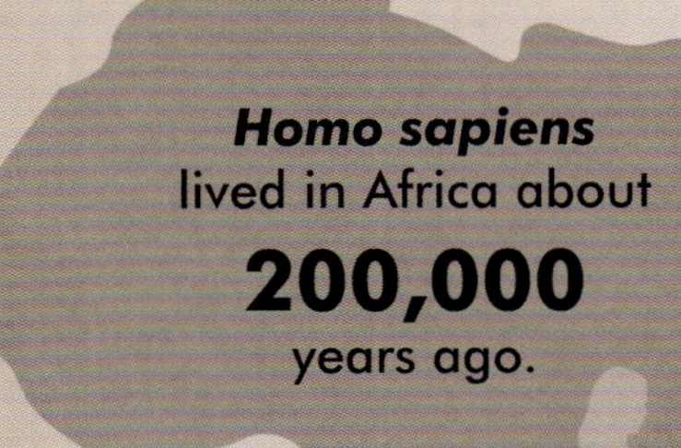

Homo sapiens **MIGRATED** (= moved from one part of the world to another)...

... probably **100,000** years ago

and **60,000** years ago.

Homo sapiens settled down and started farming about **12,000** years ago.

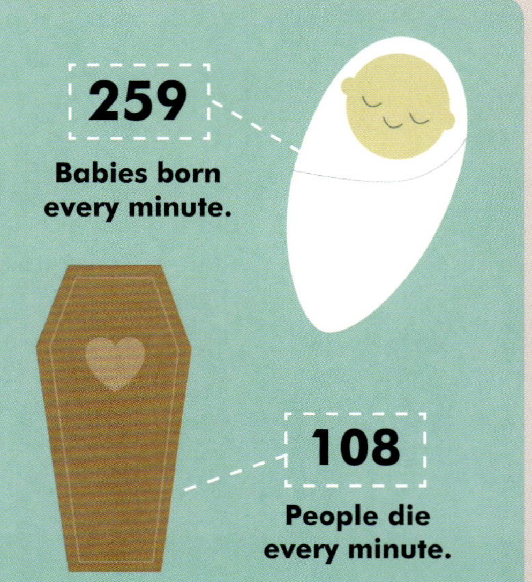

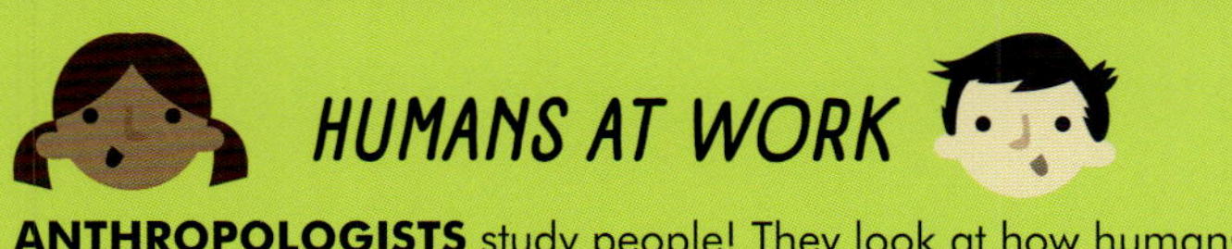

HUMANS AT WORK

ANTHROPOLOGISTS study people! They look at how humans behave and live, from prehistoric times to today.

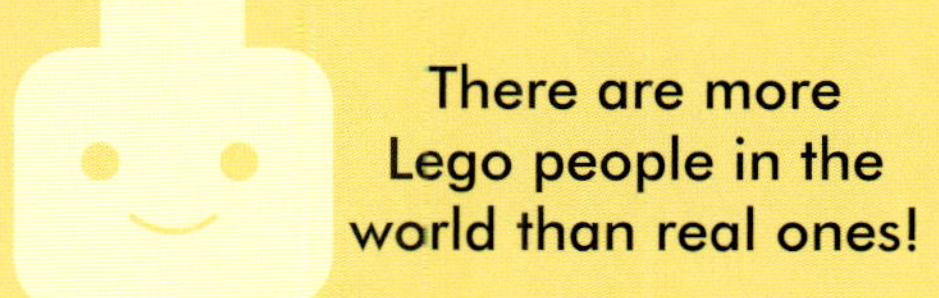

There are more Lego people in the world than real ones!

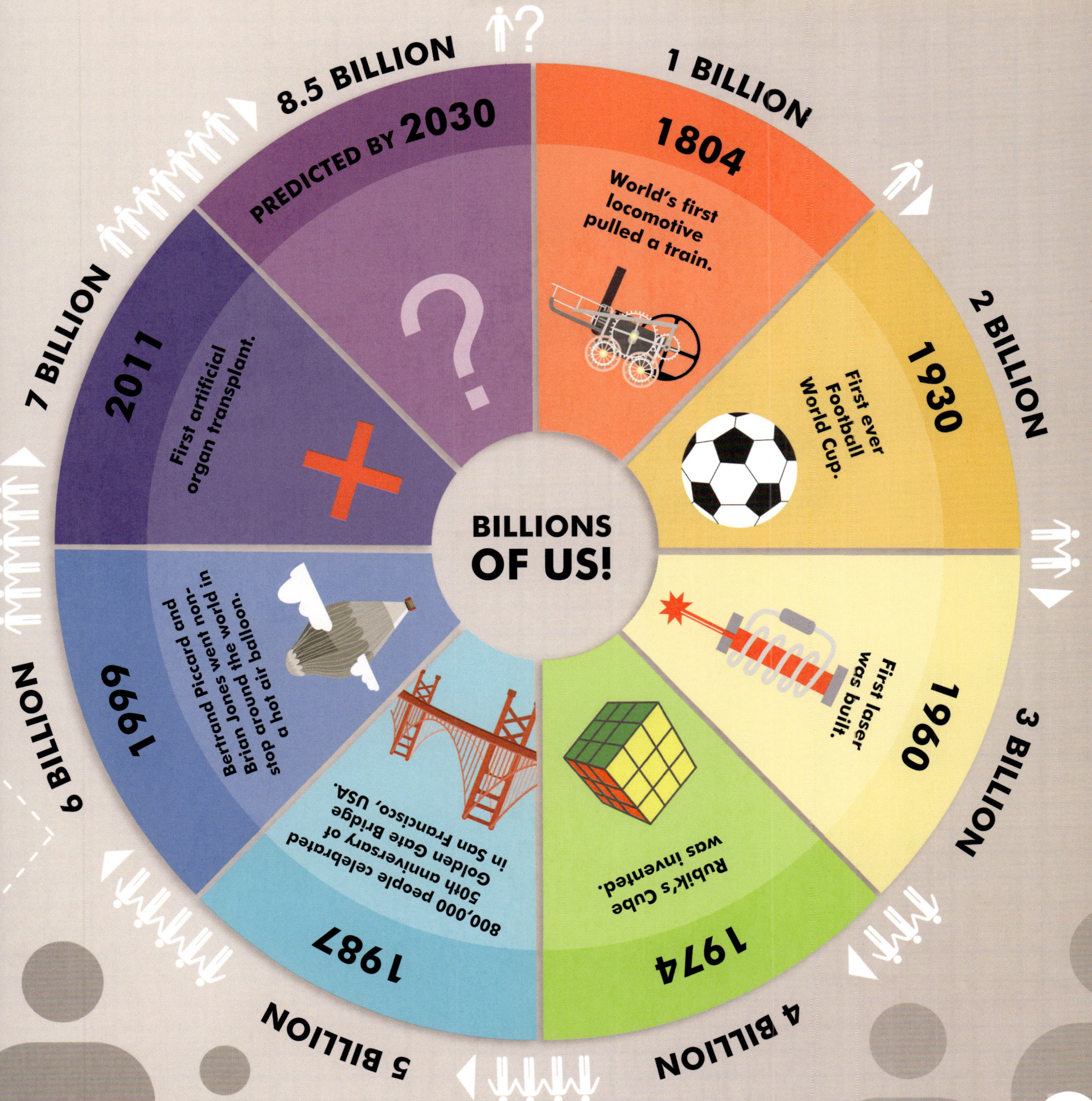

BILLIONS OF US!

1 BILLION — **1804** World's first locomotive pulled a train.

2 BILLION — **1930** First ever Football World Cup.

3 BILLION — **1960** First laser was built.

4 BILLION — **1974** Rubik's Cube was invented.

5 BILLION — **1987** 800,000 people celebrated 50th anniversary of Golden Gate Bridge in San Francisco, USA.

6 BILLION — **1999** Bertrand Piccard and Brian Jones went non-stop around the world in a hot air balloon.

7 BILLION — **2011** First artificial organ transplant.

8.5 BILLION — **PREDICTED BY 2030** ?

WHERE WE LIVE

We are so lucky to have such a beautiful planet to live on. Humans make homes in all sorts of places on Earth, but if you look at the planet at night from space you can see where most of us live by looking at the lit-up areas.

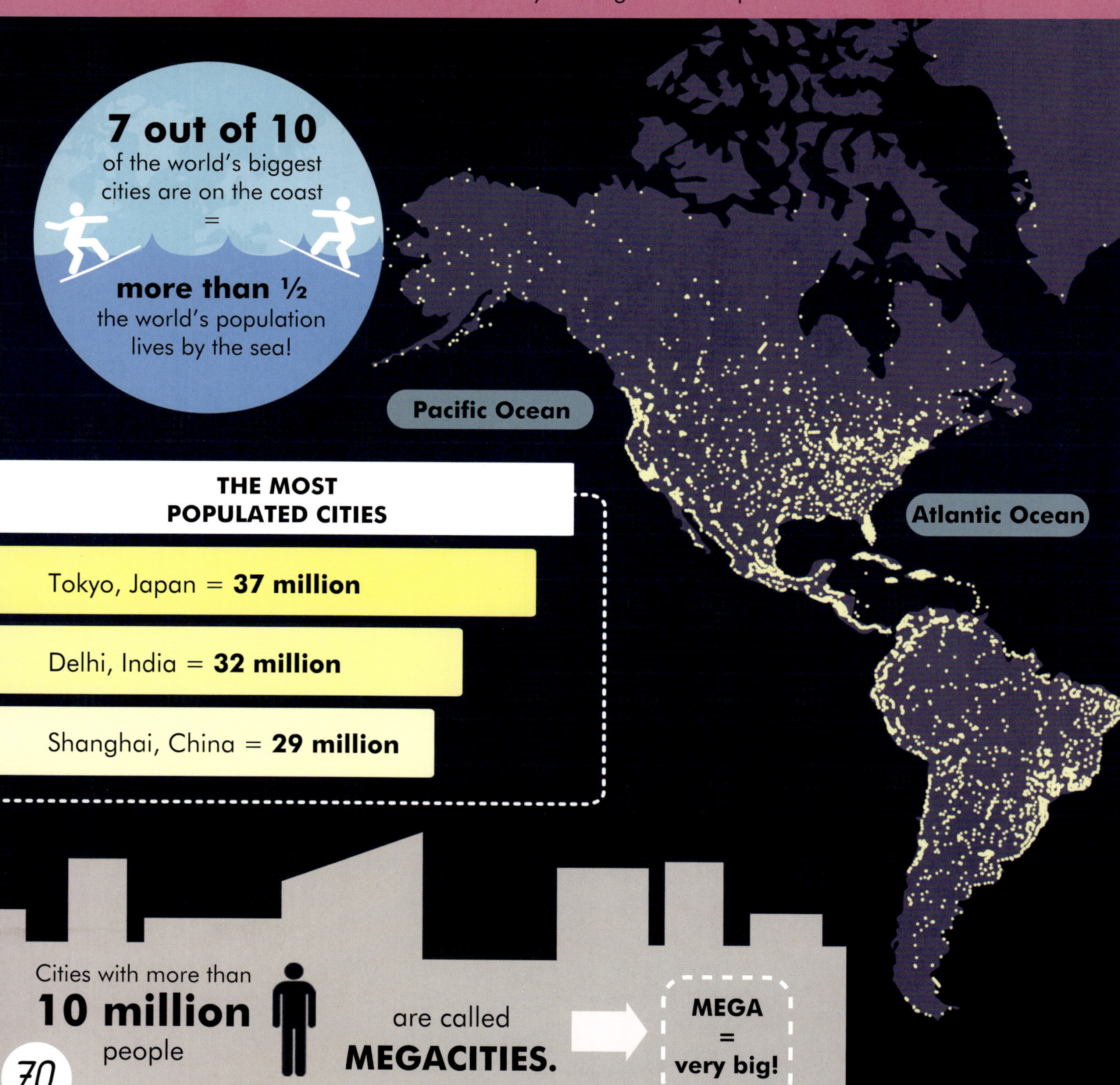

7 out of 10 of the world's biggest cities are on the coast = **more than ½** the world's population lives by the sea!

THE MOST POPULATED CITIES

- Tokyo, Japan = **37 million**
- Delhi, India = **32 million**
- Shanghai, China = **29 million**

Cities with more than **10 million** people are called **MEGACITIES.**

MEGA = very big!

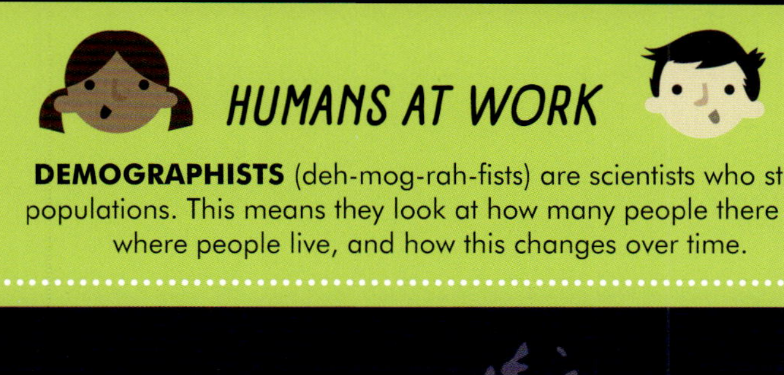

HUMANS AT WORK

DEMOGRAPHISTS (deh-mog-rah-fists) are scientists who study populations. This means they look at how many people there are, where people live, and how this changes over time.

GREENLAND is the **BIGGEST** island in the world but **LEAST** populated country **(About 56,500 people).**

JAPAN is DENSELY populated = **879 people** per square mile.

No one lives in the middle of the **SAHARA DESERT!**

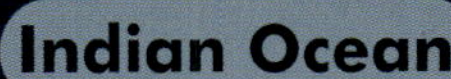

ANTARCTICA
Loads of penguins (and a few visiting scientists).

WATER TO DRINK

Humans need water and not just any old water. We need safe, clean water to stay healthy. Have you ever thought about where your water comes from and how much of it you use each day?

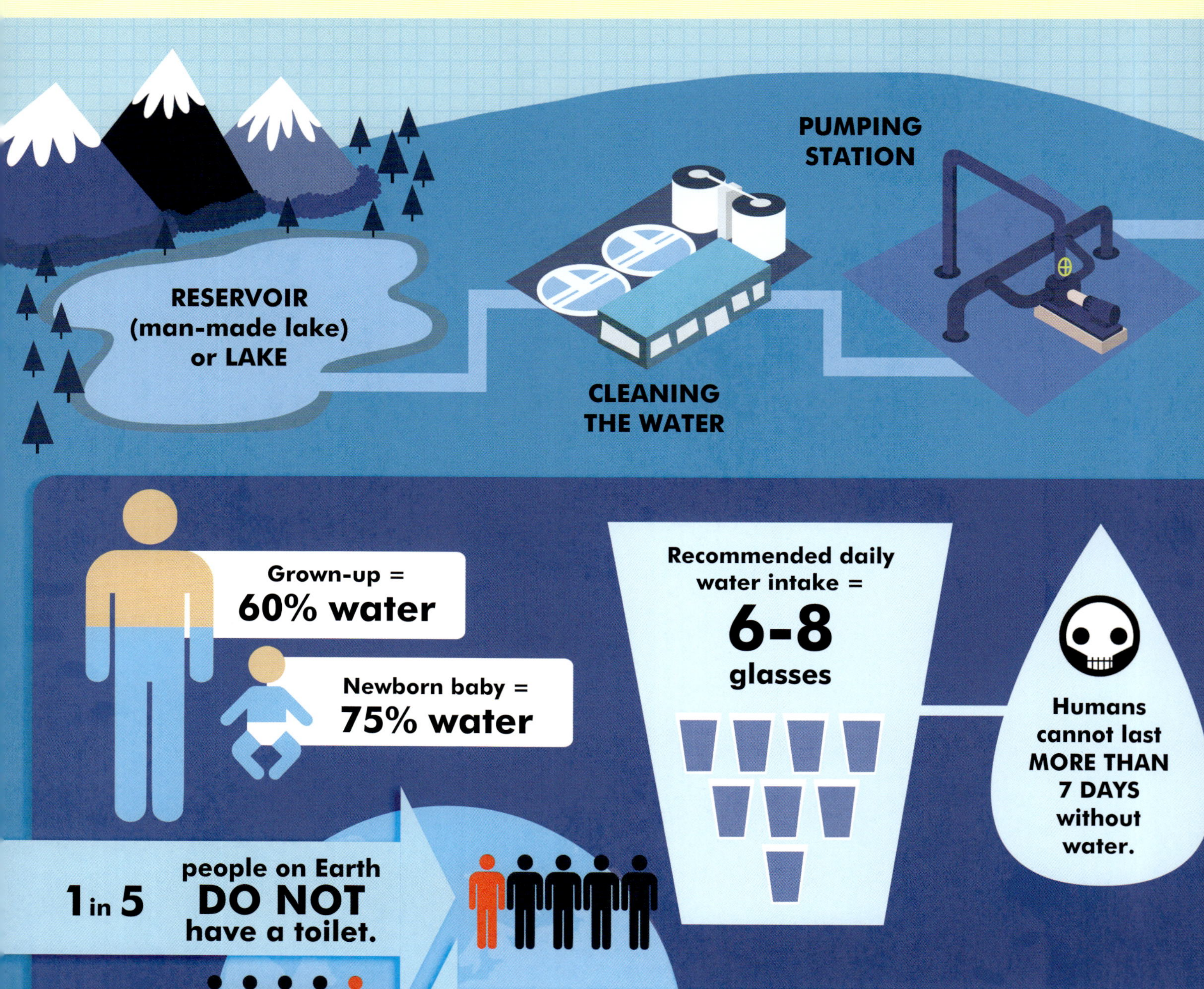

HUMANS AT WORK

WATER CONSERVATIONISTS work to protect water supplies in the environment. They help to make sure that water is used carefully. It is too precious to waste!

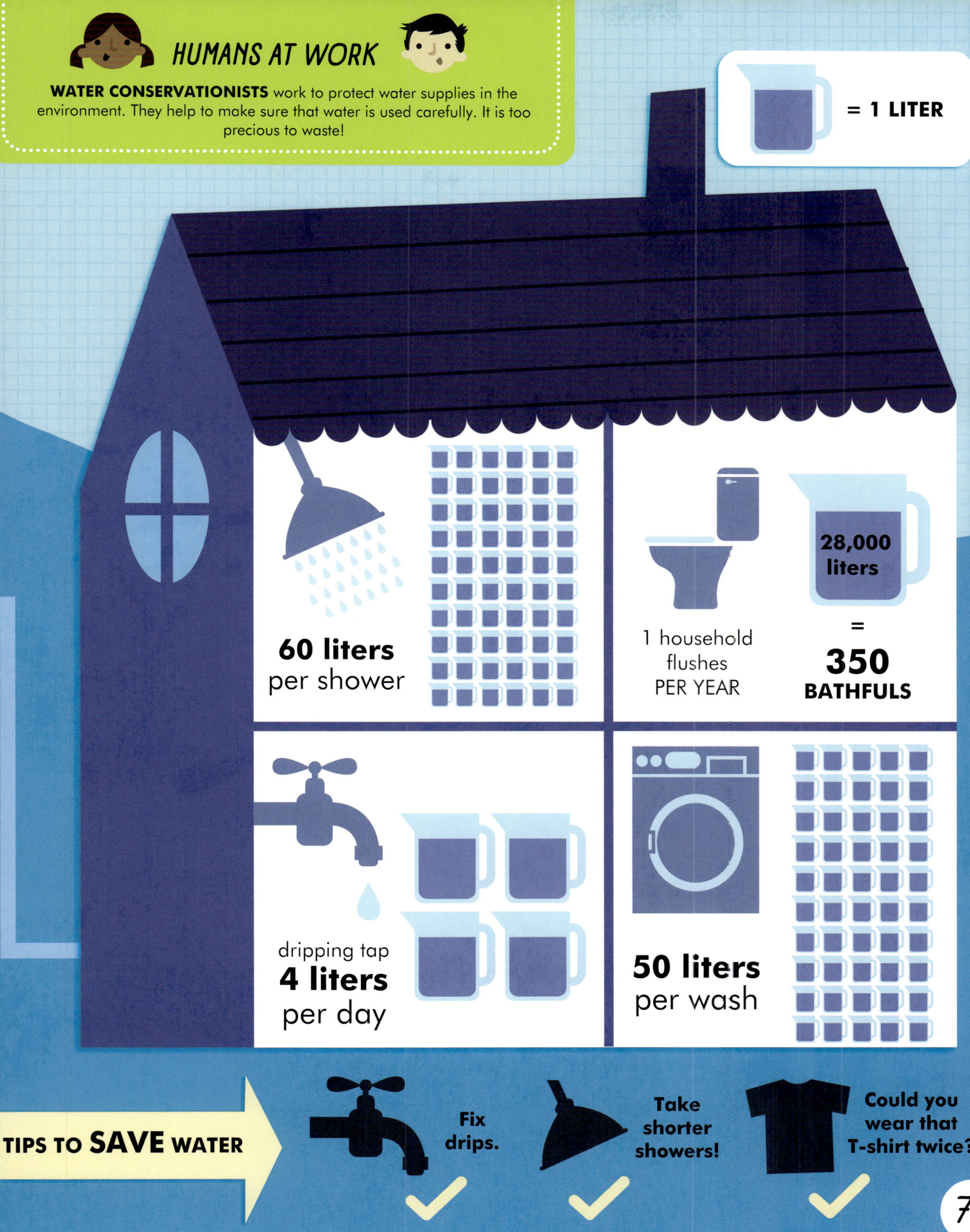

GETTING AROUND

Humans have invented many different ways to travel. We can fly far across the planet in a plane or take to the seas in a ship. We can whiz around on bicycles, motorbikes or in cars. Imagine how long it might take to go right around the world using different forms of transport.

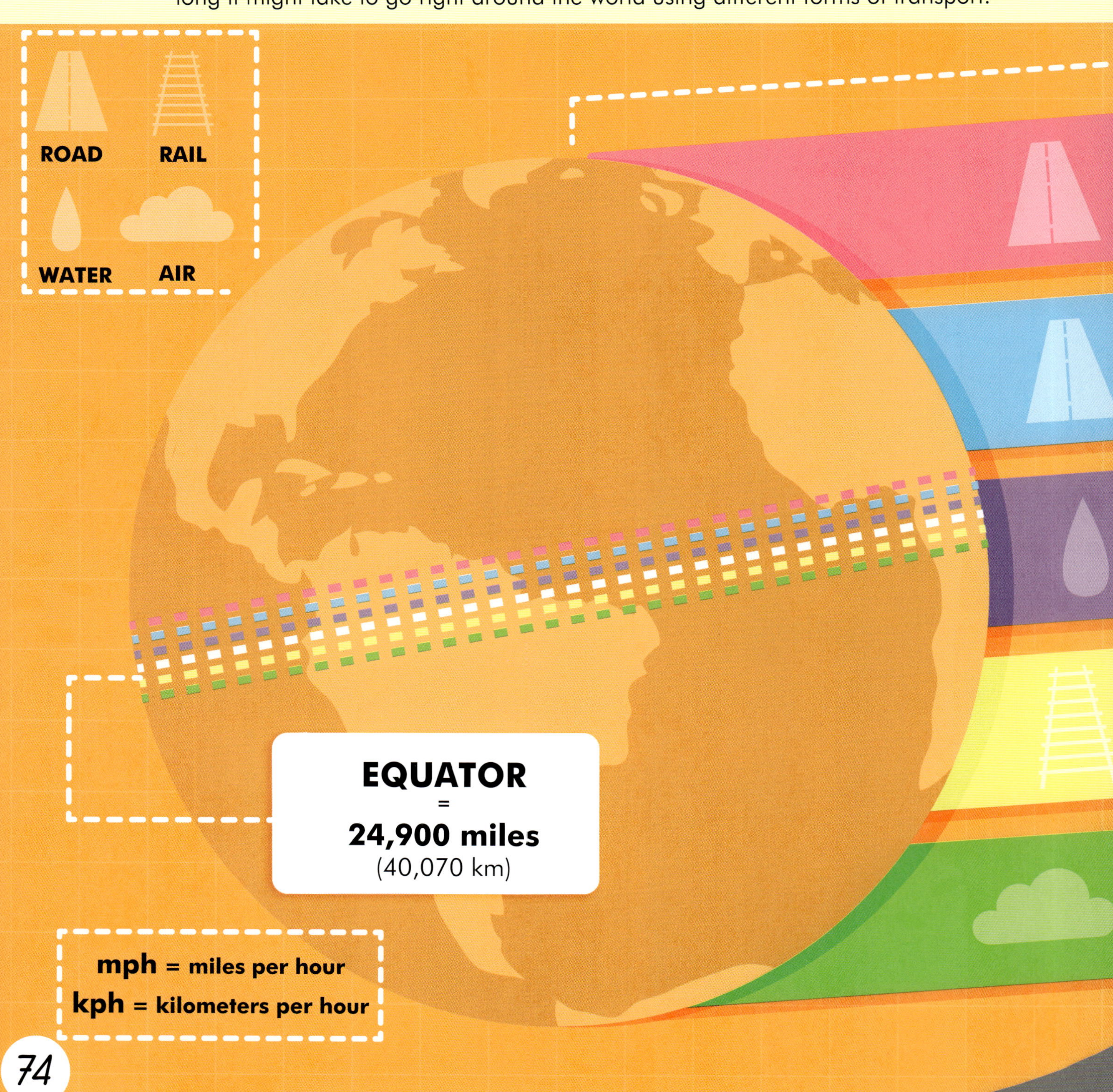

HUMANS AT WORK

ENGINEERS use science to solve problems, like how to invent the fastest train. **ASTRONAUTS** are trained to travel into space to do research and explore the Universe.

Earth to Mars
= 34 million miles
(55 million km)

No human has been there yet!

6 mph (10 kph) **TAKES 167 days**

60 mph (100 kph) **TAKES 17 days**

23 mph (37 kph) **TAKES 45 days**

A ship's speed is measured in KNOTS.

1 KNOT = 1.15 mph (1.8 kph)

60 mph (100 kph) **TAKES 17 days**

550 mph (885 kph) **TAKES under 2 days**

FASTEST TRAIN ON WHEELS

French TGV150

Top Speed = 355 mph (574 kph)

AMPHIBIOUS VEHICLES
These can go on land and sea.

TRASH!

Dumping trash and waste on land or in rivers and seas pollutes our world. This then harms people, animals and plants. We only have one planet and we all need to look after it carefully.

We **CHUCK IT** in the **BIN** and **FORGET** about it **BUT**...

PILES OF TRASH

There are millions of tons of trash in landfill.

Some never rots.

Some rots and gives off nasty gases.

This damages the atmosphere.

Plastic in landfill takes **500 YEARS** to rot away (decompose).

PLASTIC IN THE SEA

Plastic dumped in the sea poisons or traps fish and sea animals.

BIGGEST PLASTIC ISLAND

=

Pacific Garbage Patch in Pacific Ocean.

It is **3 x** the size of **France...**

This is the same as

250 PIECES of trash

for **EVERY PERSON** in the world.

... and weighs same as

500 JUMBO JETS!

HUMANS AT WORK

PRODUCT DESIGNERS design all the things we use in our lives, from chairs to computers and toothbrushes to schoolbags! Many designers try to make sure that their designs use recycled materials.

THINK BEFORE YOU CHUCK IT OUT! Can it be recycled or reused?

TAKE ACTION!

Use your own bags.

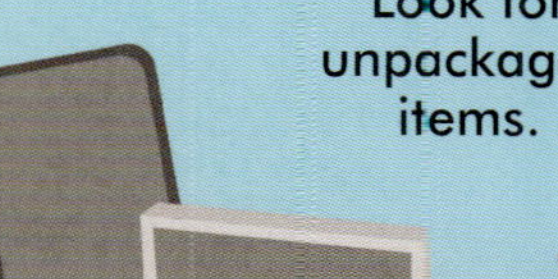

Look for unpackaged items.

Buy refills.

Find out which charities recycle old mobile phones or computers.

Don't buy too much stuff, like food, in the first place!

RECYCLING

25 x 2-liter plastic bottles makes

1 fleece.

1 tonne of **RECYCLED PAPER** saves

17 TREES.

FOOD CANS ARE **100% RECYCLABLE.**

GLASS IS **100% RECYCLABLE.**

COMPOSTING

turns kitchen and garden waste into food for plants.

peels

old fruit

teabags

uncooked veg

garden cuttings

Making **1 NEW CAN** uses the same energy as it takes to **RECYCLE 20 CANS.**

BURNING TRASH creates energy to power lights and heating... but also harmful gases.

TOP INVENTIONS

Humans are really clever and have invented so many wonderful things. It is impossible to choose the best ones, but here is a very small selection. All of them have made a big difference to our lives.

TELEPHONE

When:

1876

Who:

Alexander Graham Bell

Life-changer:

Humans can now talk to people who are not in the same room.

Fun fact:

The first mobile phones were made in the 1970s.

WATERPROOF CLOTHING

When:

1823

Who:

Charles Macintosh

Life-changer:

Humans can keep warm and dry, whatever the weather.

Fun fact:

Raincoats are still sometimes called Mackintoshes or Macs.

PETROL CAR

When:

1885

Who:

Karl Benz

Life-changer:

Humans can now really go places! But...

Fun fact:

Benz's first car only had three wheels!

HUMANS AT WORK

An **INVENTOR** is someone who comes up with an idea for a new gadget or a way of doing things. They can get a special license to stop other people pinching their ideas! This is called a **PATENT**.

AIRPLANE

When:

1903

Who:

Orville and Wilbur Wright

Life-changer:

Humans can now fly!

Fun fact:

Their first flight = **120 feet (36 meters)** in **12 SECONDS**.

POP-UP TOASTER

When:

1921

Who:

Charles Strite

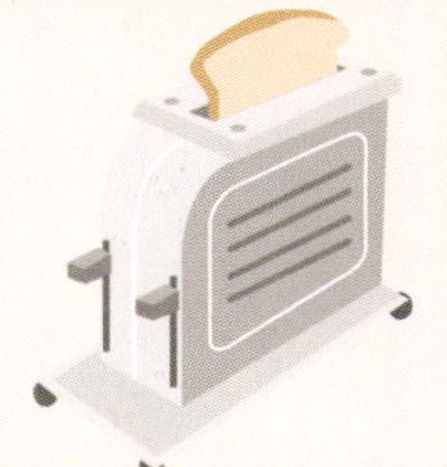

SLICED BREAD

When:

1928

Who:

Otto Rohwedder

Life-changer:

Human breakfasts are never the same again!

Fun fact:

By 1933 **8** out of **10** loaves in the USA were **SLICED.**

VACUUM-CLEANER

When:

1901

Who:

Hubert Cecil Booth

Life-changer:

Humans can clean their homes quickly and easily.

Fun fact:

The first vacuum cleaner was called PUFFING BILLY. It was so **BIG** it had to be pulled from house to house!

A BIOME TO CALL HOME

Planet Earth is home to millions of animals. The world has many types of land and climate, from freezing cold mountains to wet and hot forests. These different areas are called biomes. Let's have a look at some of them and the animals who live there.

DESERTS

Have less than **10 inches** **(25 cm)** rain **EACH YEAR.**

HOTTEST desert air temperature

134°F (56.7°C)

was recorded in Death Valley, USA.

The Antarctic and Arctic are **COLD DESERTS.**

POLAR ZONES

Arctic

Antarctica

It is **DARK** for **6 MONTHS** a year.

The air is so **COLD** your breath makes **ICE CRYSTALS.**

ANTARCTICA
There are no land animals here BUT lots in the ocean.

WETLANDS

This is land that is **ALWAYS** covered by **WATER,**

like **BOGS, SWAMPS** and **MARSHES.**

FRESH or **SALT**

BRACKISH
(a mixture of fresh and salt)

Wetlands are essential snack bars for **1,000s** of migrating birds.

WORKING WITH ANIMALS

A **HABITAT SPECIALIST** works in wildlife parks and zoos to make sure that animals have the surroundings and homes they need. They can help to set up safe places for endangered creatures, too.

Animals can be **VERTEBRATES** or **INVERTEBRATES**

= Animals with a backbone.

= Animals without a backbone.

97% of animals are invertebrates.

TROPICAL RAINFORESTS

These are found between the Tropic of Cancer and the Tropic of Capricorn.

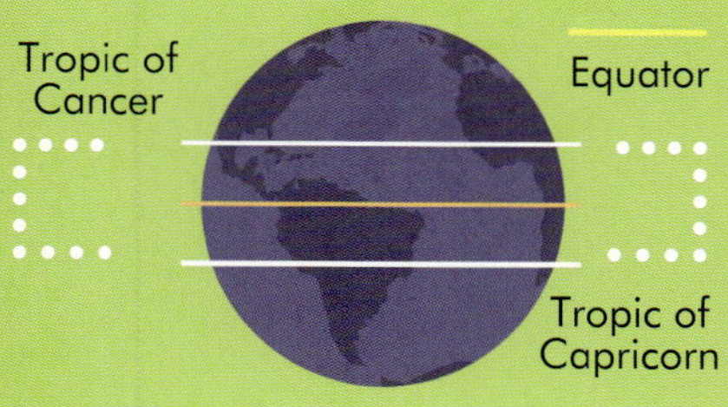

There is more rain here in **2 DAYS** than there is in a desert in **1 YEAR.**

More than **HALF** of **ALL** animal species live here.

GRASSLANDS

These have more rain than deserts, but not enough to grow many trees.

Grasslands have the **LARGEST** herds of animals, **BIGGEST** and **FASTEST** land animals and **BIGGEST** birds on Earth.

MOUNTAINS

It gets **COLDER** and **COLDER** as you go up a mountain.

EVERY 3,280 feet (1,000 m) UP = **50°F (10°C) drop.**

There are also **STRONG** winds

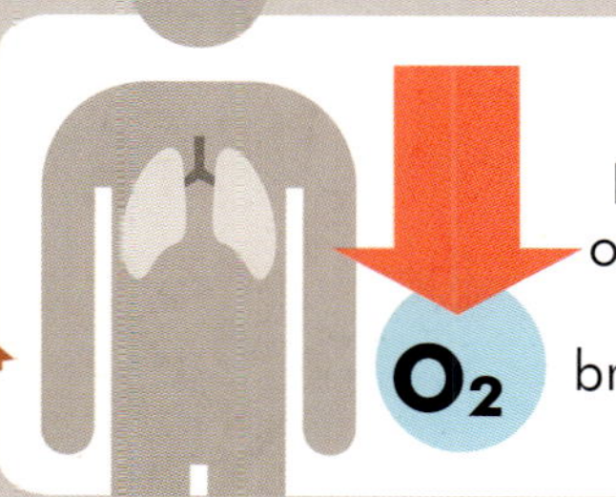

and **LESS** oxygen to breathe.

Ibex

Golden eagle

Mountain lion

Alpine marmot

ANIMAL LIVES

Some animals live for much longer than others. Animals in zoos and pet animals usually live longer than the ones in the wild. All animals have babies. Some babies grow inside the mother animal's body before being born alive. Other animals lay eggs with babies inside them.

	GESTATION or INCUBATION	NUMBER OF BABIES
LONG-TAILED SHREW	21 days (3 weeks)	2-5 babies
DOG	2 months (9 weeks)	3-6 puppies (but sometimes can be up to 10!)
HORSE	11 months	1 foal
POLAR BEAR	8 months	2 cubs (stay with mom for up to 3 years)
BOTTLENOSE DOLPHIN	1 year	1 calf
AFRICAN ELEPHANT	22 months	1 calf
GIANT TORTOISE	babies hatch out after 8 months	lays 25 eggs

WORKING WITH ANIMALS

VETERINARY SURGEONS and **VETERINARY NURSES** look after animals when they are sick or need an operation. They might work with pets like dogs, cats and hamsters, or treat animals like rhinos and giraffes in wildlife reserves.

Elephant babies stay with their mums for

This is longer than any other animals apart from humans!

The Greenland shark is **OVOVIVIPAROUS**

=

eggs hatch INSIDE the mother shark and then the baby sharks are born.

10 pups

might live up to 400 YEARS!

AVERAGE LIFE SPAN

18 MONTHS

8-15 YEARS

25-30 YEARS

25-30 YEARS

up to 45 YEARS

70 YEARS

up to 200 YEARS!

AMAZING MIGRATIONS

Some animals go on very long journeys every year. These journeys are called migrations. Some animals migrate to search for food or warmer weather. Others travel vast distances to have their babies in the same place every year.

WORKING WITH ANIMALS

ORNITHOLOGISTS study everything to do with birds. They sometimes work in very wild places to research bird migrations, nesting habits and bird life cycles. You can be a bird scientist yourself with a pair of binoculars and lots of patience!

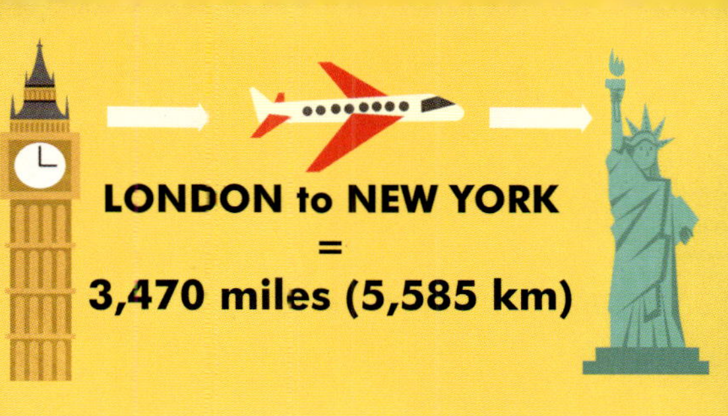

WILDEBEEST

are also called gnus (ger-noos).

Their **CIRCULAR ROUTE** in East Africa is called **THE GREAT MIGRATION.**

TOTAL round trip = **1,800 miles** (2,900 km)

2 MILLION wildebeest on the move.

They can run as fast as **50 mph** (80 kph).

GREY WHALES

Migrate from the Arctic to Mexico and back again.

RETURN trip for **ADULT WHALES** = **10,000 miles** (16,000 km)

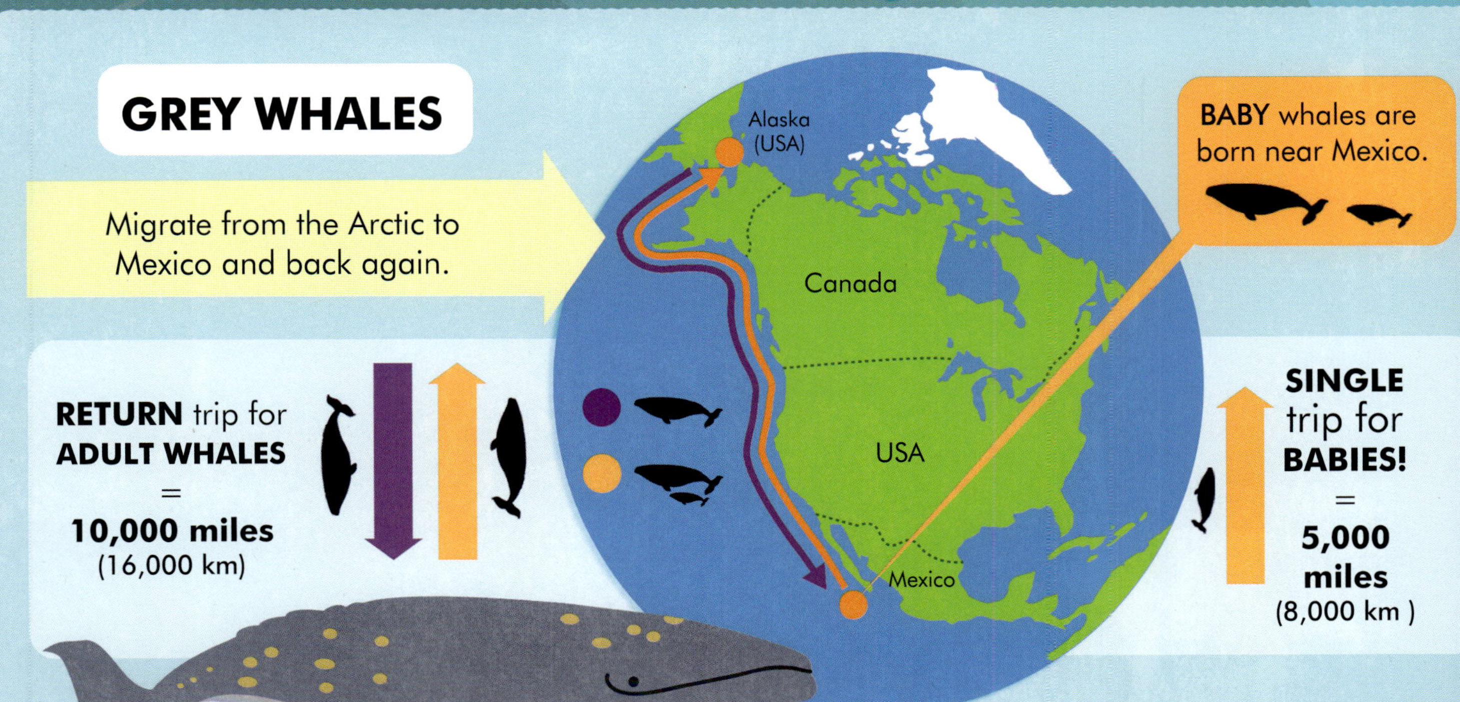

BABY whales are born near Mexico.

SINGLE trip for **BABIES!** = **5,000 miles** (8,000 km)

TREASURE ISLANDS

Some places on Planet Earth are home to very special animals. These creatures cannot be found anywhere else in the world. They are called 'native', or 'endemic', species. One of these amazing places is an island called Madagascar. But how did these animals get there in the first place?

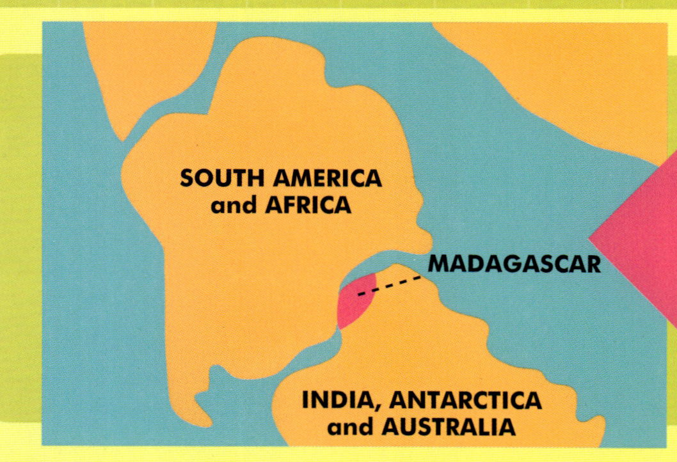

160 MILLION years ago

There was a huge supercontinent called Gondwana. The land that became Madagascar was inside it.

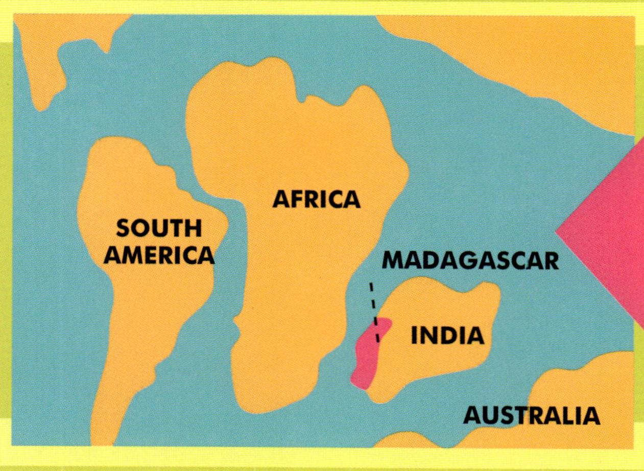

100 MILLION years ago

Madagascar was still joined to India.

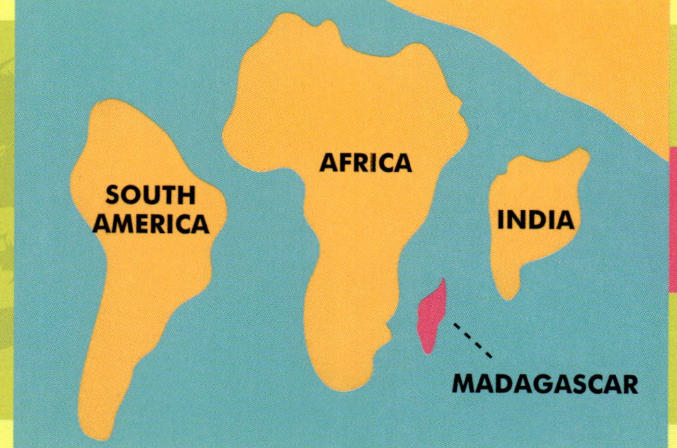

60 MILLION years ago

Madagascar became an island!

WORKING WITH ANIMALS

WILDLIFE FILM-MAKERS make films about animals. They can show us so much about animals we might never see in the wild ourselves. They can also show us how humans damage or hurt animals by destroying their homes or hunting them.

Madagascar's animals **EITHER**

stayed on for the ride as the land broke apart and moved.

Giant elephant bird = now **EXTINCT.**

OR

crossed to Madagascar from Africa **54 MILLION** years ago.

Lemurs still live on the island and **NOWHERE ELSE.**

Now **4th largest** island in the world **248 miles** (400 km) off the coast of Africa.

Giraffe weevil

Other **NATIVE** animals on Madagascar

Fossa is as **long** as a man is **tall.**

TOP PREDATOR on the island and it eats lemurs!

Mini-chameleon can fit on a fingertip!

SKY ISLANDS

In some parts of the world, like Mozambique in Africa, there are forests on the tops of mountains. These are like islands in the sky, containing many unique animal treasures. It's very hard to get to them so the native animals have been able to stay hidden and safe – for now.

MINI-WORLDS

The different biomes of the world contain lots of ecosystems. An ecosystem is like a neighborhood of animals and plants who rely on each other to survive. A healthy ecosystem has loads of different animals and plants living in it. Ecologists use grids called quadrats to count and measure the creatures living in one small area of an ecosystem.

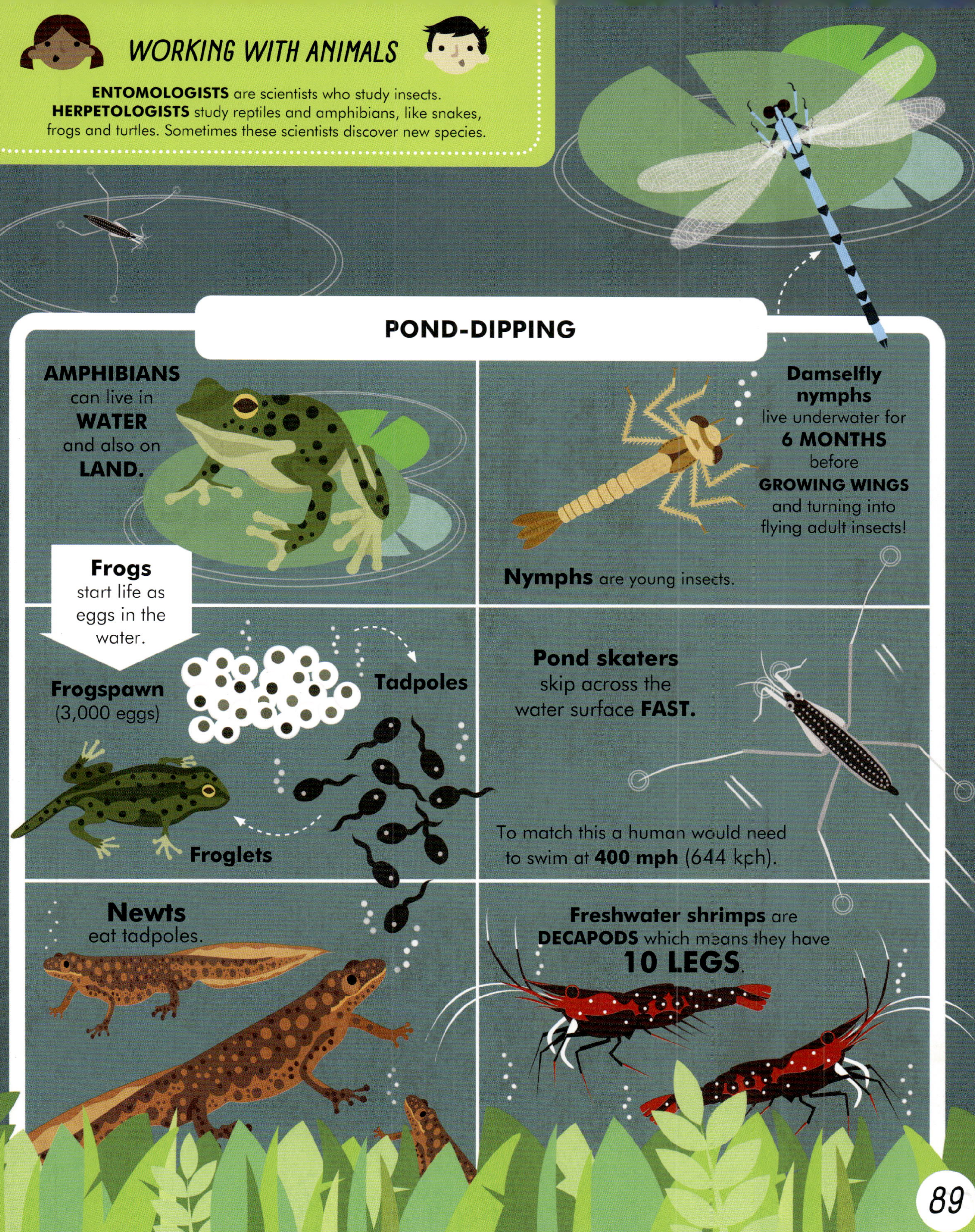
WORKING WITH ANIMALS
ENTOMOLOGISTS are scientists who study insects. **HERPETOLOGISTS** study reptiles and amphibians, like snakes, frogs and turtles. Sometimes these scientists discover new species.
POND-DIPPING
AMPHIBIANS can live in **WATER** and also on **LAND.**
Damselfly nymphs live underwater for **6 MONTHS** before **GROWING WINGS** and turning into flying adult insects!
Nymphs are young insects.
Frogs start life as eggs in the water.
Frogspawn (3,000 eggs)
Tadpoles
Froglets
Pond skaters skip across the water surface **FAST.**
To match this a human would need to swim at **400 mph** (644 kph).
Newts eat tadpoles.
Freshwater shrimps are **DECAPODS** which means they have **10 LEGS**.

HELPFUL ANIMALS

All animals were wild to start with, but humans have tamed (or domesticated) some of them. For example, some animals are kept on farms so that they can provide us with meat, milk or eggs. The first animal that humans tamed thousands of years ago was the dog.

15,000 - 36,000 years ago (Scientists cannot be more precise yet!)

12,000 years ago

People began to farm.

36,000 years ago | **30,000** | **25,000** | **20,000** | **15,000**

People were building shelters with branches, bones and skins.

DOGS ON DUTY

Sniffer dogs are trained to find illegal drugs, guns or missing people.

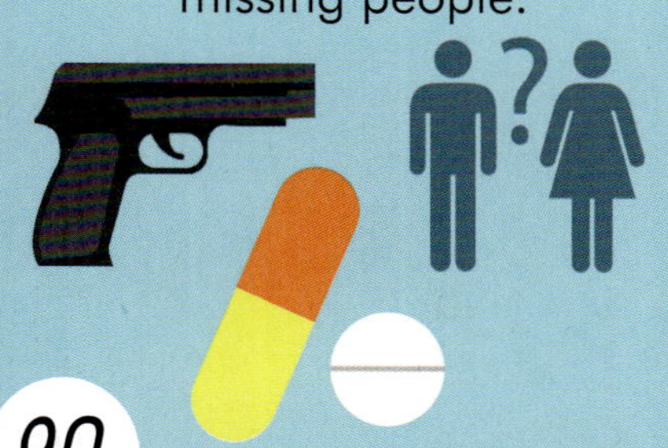

Guide and hearing dogs are trained to help blind or deaf people get out and about.

WORKING WITH ANIMALS

ANIMAL TRAINERS prepare animals for all sorts of jobs, from helping people with disabilities to detective work. The trainer must make sure that the animal understands exactly what to do when it hears or sees certain commands.

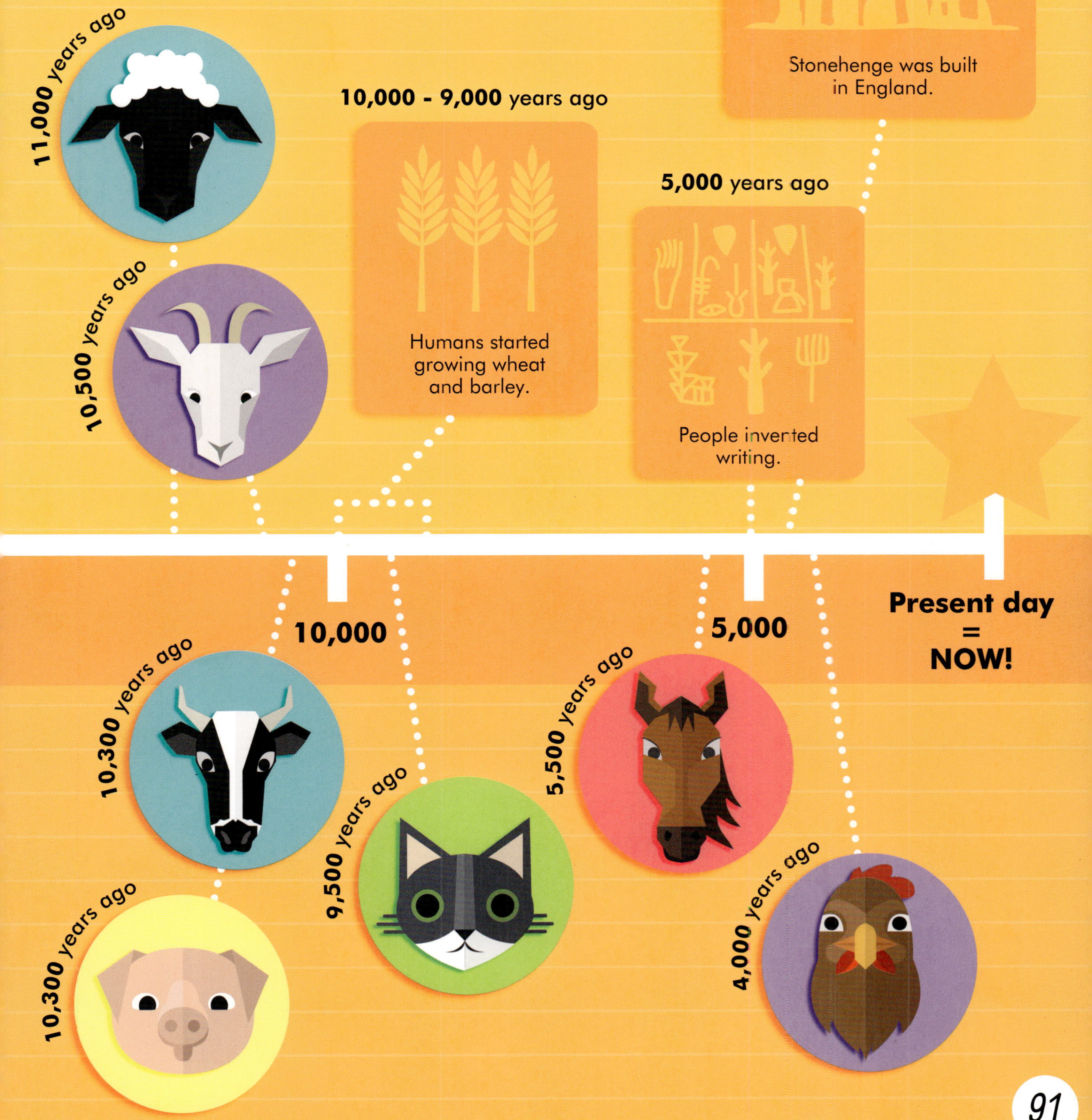

About 4,500 years ago

Stonehenge was built in England.

11,000 years ago

10,500 years ago

10,000 - 9,000 years ago

Humans started growing wheat and barley.

5,000 years ago

People invented writing.

10,000

5,000

Present day = NOW!

10,300 years ago

10,300 years ago

9,500 years ago

5,500 years ago

4,000 years ago

SAVE US!

Many animal species are in danger of dying out completely because humans are destroying so many of the places where they live. Some animals are also in danger because people hunt them for their horns, tusks or meat. We need to take urgent action to save them.

SINCE 1970

The **TOTAL NUMBER** of **wild animals with backbones** (vertebrates) has gone down by **nearly 70%**.

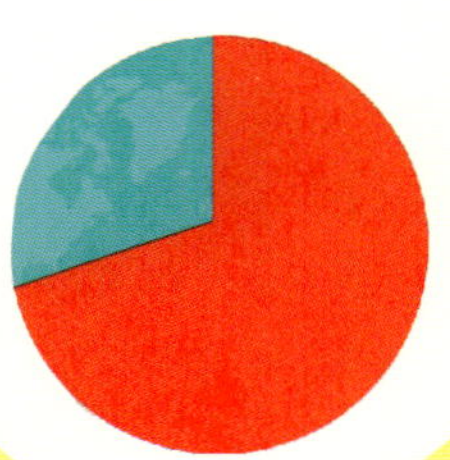

Freshwater vertebrates down by **83%**.

ONE THIRD of sharks and rays are at risk of extinction.

PANGOLINS

8 species in the world.

Hunted for their scales and meat.

AFRICAN ELEPHANTS

The **LARGEST** animals walking the Earth.

Live in **37** countries in Africa.

SUMATRAN TIGERS

Found only on the Indonesian island of Sumatra.

WORKING WITH ANIMALS

CONSERVATIONISTS work to protect the natural habitats of animals. They often advise farmers on how to look after the wildlife on their land. **PARK RANGERS** work in parks and wildlife reserves. Sometimes they have to patrol a park to prevent illegal hunting. This is very dangerous work.

Over the last **10 YEARS** more than **1 MILLION** have been taken from the wild.

No one knows how many are left.

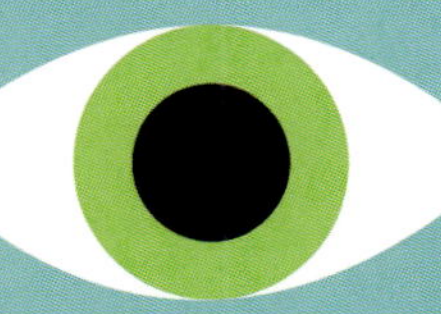

People hunt them for their ivory tusks. Their habitat is destroyed by mining and farming.

In the early **1900s** there were **3-5 MILLION** elephants.

In 1980s **100,000** elephants were killed **EACH YEAR.**

Today there are only about **415,000** elephants left.

They are hunted and their forest home is being destroyed.

1978 **1,000** tigers

2018 fewer than **400** tigers

40 tigers are **KILLED EVERY YEAR.**

TAKE ACTION!

Look up information about animals in danger and how to help on the websites of conservation charities like the World Wide Fund for Nature.

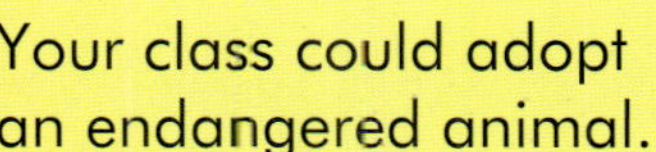

Your class could adopt an endangered animal.

Help spread the message about how important it is to share our planet with animals and keep them safe.

WORDS TO KNOW

ACTIVE
An active volcano is one that might erupt. It could chuck out lots of hot, melted rock (magma).

ANIMAL
A living thing that breathes. It can also move around to find food for itself. The Latin word anima means 'breath' or 'spirit'.

ARTIFICIAL
means something made by humans. An artificial organ is a copy of the real thing.

ATMOSPHERE
is the air all around Planet Earth. It is made of different layers.

AXIS
The Earth's axis is an imaginary line drawn between the North and South Poles. The Earth tilts slightly on its axis.

BILLION
is a thousand million or 1,000,000,000.

BIOME
A large area of Planet Earth that has a certain climate and types of living things in it. Examples of biomes are grasslands, deserts or forests.

CARBON DIOXIDE (CO_2)
A type of gas in the Earth's atmosphere. It is also the gas we breathe out and that plants and trees breathe in.

CLIMATE
The usual weather in an area of the world. It takes many years, even thousands of years, to change. It is not the same as weather, which can change from day to day.

CONSERVATION
means trying to protect wild animals and their habitats.

CONTINENT
A very large area of land.

DECIDUOUS
Deciduous trees lose their leaves in autumn and grow new ones in the spring.

DECOMPOSE
means to rot away. Dead things and rubbish decompose.

DOMESTICATE
means to tame an animal to keep it as a pet or on a farm.

ECOSYSTEM
This is like a neighborhood where everything has an important place of its own. It is made up of not only all the living things there, but also includes things like the weather, rocks, soil or sand.

ENDANGERED
means animals that are in danger of dying out or becoming extinct.

ENDEMIC
describes animals that live in a particular area of the world, like the unique species in Madagascar.

ENVIRONMENT
is the air, water or land that people and animals live in or on.

EQUATOR
is an imaginary line that runs around the middle, or 'waist', of the Earth.

EVERGREEN
Evergreen trees and plants do not lose their leaves in autumn. They stay green all year.

EVOLUTION
The theory that says all living things alive today developed (or evolved) from earlier versions that lived billions of years ago.

EXTINCT
An animal that has died out is extinct. It means that there is not even one of them left alive anywhere in the world.

GALAXY
A huge collection of stars and planets. The Universe contains billions of galaxies.

GESTATION
is the length of time that a mammal carries her babies inside her body before they are born.

HABITAT
is where animals live and make their homes. Animals can live in all kinds of habitats from boiling hot to freezing cold places.

HOMO SAPIENS
This is the name given to our own modern human species.

INCUBATION
is the length of time it takes for baby creatures to be ready to hatch out of eggs.

INVERTEBRATE
A creature without a backbone or spine. Insects are invertebrates.

LANDFILL
is another word for a rubbish dump or tip.

MAMMAL
is an animal that breathes air, has a backbone and produces milk to feed its babies. It also grows hair or fur at some point in its life.

MEGACITY
A megacity has more than 10 million people living in it.

MIGRATE
means to travel from one area to another, sometimes over very long distances.

MIGRATION
The journey made every year by some animals. They travel to and from feeding and breeding habitats.

MINERALS
are crystals inside rocks. They are like the 'building blocks' of rocks.

MOLTEN
means melted into liquid.

ORBIT
means to circle around something. Planet Earth orbits the Sun.

OXYGEN (O_2)
A gas in the atmosphere that humans and many living things need to breathe.

OZONE
A gas in the atmosphere that helps to absorb most of the harmful rays of the Sun.

PHOTOSYNTHESIS
is how plants and trees use sunshine, water and carbon dioxide to make food for themselves.

POLLUTION
is when poisonous or harmful stuff is put into the environment.

POPULATION
is the number of people in a town, country or the world.

PRESSURE
is when something pushes or presses down or against something else.

RADIUS
A straight line from the center to the edge of a circle or sphere.

RECYCLE
means to reuse something by making it into something else instead of throwing it away.

RESPIRATION
is the scientific name for breathing.

ROTATE
means to make a circle, or rotation, around an axis or center.

SHOCK WAVE
A sudden wave of very high pressure moving through the air, earth or water. It is caused by earthquakes or explosions.

SPECIES
A group of animals or plants that are similar.

TECTONIC
means to do with the Earth's crust, how it is formed and how it is still changing.

TEMPERATE
means not too hot and not too cold.

TROPICAL
Tropical areas are just to the north and south of the Equator. They are very hot and wet.

UNIVERSE
The name given to everything that exists in space and time.

VERTEBRATE
is an animal with a backbone or spine.